I0520612

The Internal Revolution

Lead Authentically and
Build Your Personal Brand
from Within

Dana Williams

Authentic Imprint Publishing
Copyright ©2025 Dana Williams
www.danawilliamsco.com

ISBN 979-8-9998218-0-5

This book draws on real events, organizations, and individuals from the author's professional life. To respect privacy or at the request of those involved, names and identifying details have been changed or omitted, and some accounts have been combined or altered. The perspectives and interpretations are those of the author, based on personal recollection and professional experience. Where individuals are named, permission has been obtained, or the stories are already publicly available.

This book is intended for informational purposes only and should not be considered a substitute for professional counseling or therapy. The author is not a licensed counselor or therapist and is not providing mental health advice. Readers are encouraged to consult with a qualified professional for any specific concerns.

Printed in the United States

Produced with the assistance of Fluency Organization, Inc.
Cover Design by Inkwell Creative

Dana Williams helped Southwest become the first strengths-based airline, and now she's showing leaders everywhere how to build on that foundation. This *Internal Revolution* framework connects strengths, values, and mission in a way that transforms both leaders and organizations. Essential reading for any leader navigating change while staying true to their core.

Bob Jordan
President & Chief Executive Officer, Southwest Airlines Co.

For leaders looking to close the gap between external success and authentic impact, Dana Williams' Internal Revolution framework is the answer. Her emphasis on starting with inner change is essential to building a magnetic presence—and becoming truly unforgettable.

Lorraine K. Lee
Keynote Speaker and Bestselling Author of *Unforgettable Presence*

In the business of creativity, I've learned that transformative client partnerships and record-breaking results flow from leaders who do the internal work in addition to the professional work. Dana Williams brilliantly connects authentic self-discovery to powerful external impact. This book is essential for any leader ready to build brands—including their own—from the inside out.

Marianne Malina
North America President, 72andSunny

Dana Williams addresses the leadership challenge I see every day—leaders who've achieved external success but lost their 'gusto' for authentic impact. This Internal Revolution framework bridges the gap between who leaders think they should be and who they're called to be. Essential reading for any leader ready to activate their organization through meaning and purpose.

Dr. Alise Cortez
Chief Ignition Officer, Gusto, Now!
Author of *The Great Revitalization: How Activating Meaning and Purpose Can Radically Enliven Your Business*
Host, Working on Purpose podcast

This book will help you establish a firm foundation and framework for being the best authentic version of yourself. Dana Williams has a gift for helping people live their strengths, dominate their day, and transform their life. Your personal happiness will grow as you unlock your best you and the gifts of those around you. Enjoy this easy-to-follow personal navigation for growth.

Bill Tierney
SVP, Marketing, Growth, & Customer Experience
Invitation Homes

I have the privilege of witnessing authentic transformation daily—watching men go from brokenness to becoming leaders of their families and communities—I understand the power of internal change. Dana Williams has created a framework that applies these same transformation principles to leadership development. Essential reading for anyone ready to rebuild their influence from the inside out.

Melinda Russ
Executive Director, Men of Nehemiah

Just as Generation Z requires leaders to evolve their approach, Dana Williams shows how authentic leadership begins with evolving ourselves first. This Internal Revolution framework helps leaders develop the character and competence needed to lead any generation effectively.

Tim Elmore
Founder, Growing Leaders, Inc.
Keynote and Workshop Speaker, Bestselling Author

I know Dana well, and I have personally learned—and continue to learn—from her wisdom, insight, and example. Like tending a garden, her process is about cultivating the right environment, planting with intention, and nurturing growth over time. Whether you're leading a team, raising a family, building a business, or simply seeking a more meaningful way forward, Dana's approach will help you uncover your own strengths, live in alignment with your values, and grow into the leader you are uniquely meant to be. This is a book you will return to again and again—not just to grow as a leader, but to grow as a person.

Donna Letier
Co-founder, Gardenuity
Mom, Wife, Friend, and Believer

As a healthcare executive, I know the demands of leading in high-stakes environments while staying true to your mission of caring for others. Dana Williams has created a framework that helps leaders maintain their authentic core while driving exceptional results. This Internal Revolution approach is essential for leaders in any industry who refuse to compromise their values for success.

Doris Hunt
Executive Vice President, Corporate Services at Children's Health

To Worth, my steadfast companion since our college days, who has never once asked me to be anyone other than who I am. Your unwavering support, endless cheering, and gentle listening have been the foundation of every brave step I've taken toward authenticity. You've shown me what it means to be truly seen and believed in—the very essence of this Internal Revolution.

To my daughter, Whitney, my greatest teacher in living fearlessly authentic. Your entrepreneurial spirit and courage to be unapologetically yourself reverse-mentors me daily, reminding me that the world doesn't need a perfect version of us—it needs the real version. Thank you for bringing Spencer into our family, a gentle soul whose peaceful presence and protective love shows us what authentic masculine leadership looks like as a husband and father to your four girls.

To my precious granddaughters—Stella, whose empathy already lights up rooms; Charlotte, whose natural gift for bringing order to chaos; Rory, whose joyful spirit keeps us all laughing; and June, whose beautiful ability to flow with life teaches us grace. You're already living your Authentic Imprints at such young ages, showing me that the Internal Revolution begins the moment we honor who we were created to be.

To my mom, who continues to teach us all that it's never too late to answer the call within, to do the impossible, and to step into the work we were created to do. Your courage to pursue purpose at every stage of life embodies the very heart of this message. To my sisters, Tracy and Beverly, and their families—may you each find your calling and live out your purpose each day.

To my stepfather, Gus, whose unwavering positivity and gift for seeing the unique spark in each of us has shaped how I understand authentic leadership. You've never missed an opportunity to listen, encourage, and root us on—never judging, never criticizing, always believing in who we're becoming. Your ability to value each person exactly as they are is the blueprint for leading from the inside out.

To Ginger Hardage, who showed me what it means to lead with grace while speaking truth with compassion. You were always there when I needed wise advice, a trusted connection, or someone who would listen and guide with genuine care. Your legacy of building authentic relationships and creating unstoppable cultures embodies the very essence of a leader.

You are all proof that when we lead from the inside out, we don't just transform our own lives—we transform everyone around us.

CONTENTS

ACKNOWLEDGEMENTS

They say it takes a village, but what they don't tell you is that the village becomes part of your Internal Revolution™. Every person mentioned here didn't just support me—they shaped who I became in the process.

To my writing partners: Mary Ann Lackland, my amazing editor and CEO of Fluency Organization, Inc., who helped transform my ideas into clear, actionable wisdom. You didn't just edit—you helped me find my voice and make this message accessible to every leader who needs it. And to Brenda Bogart, my truth-telling friend who shared her writing resources with me and was always available with insights and encouragement when I needed it most. Your belief in this message and your consistent support kept me moving forward. You embody what authentic friendship looks like.

To my Dana Williams Consulting team: This book exists because of the incredible humans who stepped into my vision and made it reality. Kristin Moore, who came alongside me and helped me launch my business during the pandemic in 2020, setting the pace for great work. Ally Willis, my Online Business Manager who brings all the talents I don't have—you are the operational genius behind everything that works. Alissa Jaquish, my partner who helps me take my ideas to frameworks and create great outcomes. Anne Murray, who went from being my best friend at work for 25 years to joining me on this entrepreneurial journey as a coach. Rachel Barnes, my IT guru and college friend who keeps all the technology humming. And Amie, my talented podcast producer who creates magic from my interviews.

But the wisdom that changed everything came from Fabienne Frederickson, my business coach, who taught me this life-altering truth: We have a five-second window to move from idea to action—our brain is wired to stop us, but when we ask for divine guidance in our business and pay attention to the signs, there are no coincidences. Fabienne, you taught me that when we're in alignment, we don't struggle. When we struggle, we're either not aligned or not listening. That became the foundation of everything you see in this book.

To my foundation: Worth, Whitney, Spencer, Mom, and Gus—you've already been honored in my dedication, but I need you to know that your daily support through this writing journey made every chapter possible. Worth, you celebrated every small win and encouraged me through every tough writing day. Whitney and Spencer, your feedback on titles, book covers, and messaging helped me stay connected to what really matters. And to my four precious granddaughters—Stella, Charlotte, Rory, and June—I see your authentic living daily and my prayer is that you never conform to the world but continue to be more of what God created you to be each day, living in your true calling. You didn't just cheer me on—you made this book better.

To my professional family: The folks at Gallup who have been unwavering supporters as I helped launch Strengths at Southwest Airlines, created The Strengths Journal™, and now brought this book to life.

To my fellow Gallup-certified CliftonStrengths Coaches who continue to show me how to turn strengths insights into real impact—thank you for the collaboration, learning, and shared commitment to helping leaders discover who they really are.

And to my Southwest Airlines family—especially the late Herb Kelleher and Colleen Barrett, along with the many leaders and friends who taught me that leadership and love aren't separate things.

To my community: My Saturday Sisters who pray and support me through everything, my CR folks—you know who you are—thank you for being part of my life each week as we do the deep work on ourselves. You have taught me so much about living in amends daily and doing the work of getting ready for eternity. My Mahjong group whose weekly time together keeps me grounded and growing my wellbeing, and Becky Lewis, who teaches me daily how to live with positivity through life's valleys while always planning the next great adventure. Becky, you encouraged me throughout writing this book and whatever I was needing, you jumped in with resources. You all remind me daily that authentic living is done in community, not in isolation.

To my clients: Thank you for entrusting my team and me to serve you. You know who you are, and you make this work pure joy. Your courage to do the internal work inspires me every single day.

To everyone mentioned here and the countless others who have been part of this journey—you didn't just help me write a book. You helped me challenge myself to be authentic every day and reminded me that the Internal Revolution is never finished—it's a daily choice to show up as who we really are.

This Internal Revolution is yours.

ABOUT THE AUTHOR

During 25 years of leadership at Southwest Airlines, Dana Williams learned that the most effective leaders don't just manage tasks—they inspire transformation. Today as an executive coach, author, and founder of Dana Williams Co., Dana helps difference makers move from performing to thriving by tapping into their authentic strengths.

Dana is a Gallup-certified CliftonStrengths expert and the creator of The Strengths Journal™—the only Gallup-certified licensed daily planning system. In addition, she is a Forbes Coaches Council member and contributor, host of the Dominate Your Day podcast, and author. *The Internal Revolution: Lead Authentically and Build Your Personal Brand from Within* is her first book. Dana's own Internal Revolution™ began during a season of profound challenge. A marriage crisis, financial devastation, and health scares taught her that lasting change only happens from the inside out. This personal breakthrough became the foundation for helping others discover their authentic leadership potential. As the visionary behind the Your Authentic Imprint™ framework, Dana has guided thousands of professionals from burnout to breakthrough.

When she's not guiding leaders through transformation, Dana can be found traveling with her husband in search of the world's best beaches, relaxing at Cedar Creek Lake near Dallas with family and friends, or exploring Dallas for the perfect Mexican food. Connect with Dana at www.danawilliamsco.com.

HOW TO USE THIS BOOK

The Internal Revolution: Lead Authentically and Build Your Personal Brand from Within is designed as both a discovery journey and a practical toolkit. Here's how to get the most from your experience with this book:

Start by Assessing

- **Authentic Imprint™ Assessment (Recommended):** Before diving into Chapter 1, consider taking the free 3-minute Authentic Imprint™ Assessment at danawilliamsco.scoreapp.com. I designed this tool to give you a baseline discovery of your authentic leadership profile and help you track your growth throughout the book.

- **CliftonStrengths Assessment (Optional):** You can also take the CliftonStrengths Assessment developed by Gallup, a global analytics and advisory firm known for its workplace research and strengths-based development. This tool helps individuals identify, understand, and maximize their strengths. If you're interested, find more information at www.danawilliamsco.com/code.

Note: Both assessments are completely optional. You do not need to take either assessment to find your strengths, complete the exercises, or benefit from this book.

Read in Chapter Order

There are three parts to this book. Each part builds on the previous one, so I encourage you to read the chapters in order.

- **Part 1 Live in Your Strengths (Chapters 1-4):** Discover your authentic foundation
- **Part 2 Dominate Your Day (Chapters 5-6):** Learn to apply what you learn daily
- **Part 3 Transform Your Life (Chapters 7-8):** Transform your relationships and impact

Engage with the Exercises

Don't just read—participate. Your Revolution callouts, questions for reflection, and the "Putting it into Practice" section at the end of each chapter are where transformation happens. Give yourself time to complete the exercises and challenges that resonate with you.

Take Your Time

While you could read this book in a weekend, living the principles is a lifetime journey. Consider reading one chapter per week and fully implementing each element before moving forward.

Connect with Our Resources on Your Journey

The work of an Internal Revolution is best done with others. Scan the QR code to connect online with Dana Williams Co. resources and follow us on social.

Your Internal Revolution starts now.

Scan for Dana Williams Co. resources.
www.danawilliamsco.com

PART 1

Live in Your Strengths

CHAPTER 1

The Archeological Dig: Uncovering Your True Self

"I don't know that person. But I'd really like to find them." Spoken more like an afterthought over a cup of coffee, the words hit me hard. I was meeting with someone who was recently separated after a long marriage steeped in co-dependency. When their spouse felt good, they felt good. When their spouse was unhappy, they'd take their emotional clues from them and were unhappy as well.

Now for the first time they had the chance to choose their own way, decide their likes and dislikes, and determine their own happiness. Instead of exploring their newfound freedom and daydreaming about what all was now possible, they were paralyzed. Total inertia. They had no idea who they really were deep inside, much less what they wanted out of life. Why? Because they had always looked outside of themselves to help determine the answers. "I don't know that person on the inside," they'd replied. "But I'd really like to find them."

What struck me most as I drove home that day was knowing how many people are looking to another person, a promotion, a title, or some elusive accomplishment to tell them who they are. Like the person I met for coffee, there's an "inner you" waiting to be revealed inside each one of us. How well do you know that person? Would you like to find them? With that discovery can come all the success and satisfaction we're all looking for in life because real change—lasting change—can only begin within.

I've coached a variety of people from executives to stay-at-home moms, and you might be surprised how many outwardly successful people still quietly struggle to know their life's greater purpose. They may have reached a certain level of accomplishment but are unsure how to tap into their life's true calling. They're sitting on the top rung of the career ladder. Or the kids are all out of the house. And their life's purpose seems to be over.

Instead of giving up, I teach them how to uncover the strengths and talents innately inside of them to help them achieve a greater sense of wellbeing and significance than they've ever experienced before. Why don't more people do this? The simple truth is that it's hard.

The level of self-discovery I'm talking about takes time. It often alters your priorities and puts much of your daily habits and schedules at an undeniable crossroads where you must choose a new path for the rest of your life. Some key relationships may change once we connect with who we really are. Some people end up moving, changing jobs, or even starting whole new careers. Doing the inner work necessary to discover who you are and what you are uniquely designed to do—and then living out what you find—does not come easily to anyone. But the rewards are amazing.

Personal Branding Pitfalls

Although there are many books about how to conduct genuine self-discovery, I believe the purpose of self-discovery is tied to personal branding. Workers in today's marketplace invest at least some, if not a lot, of time into building their personal brand at work. However, you don't have to have to have a LinkedIn profile to have a personal brand. Do moms and dads have a personal brand? Yes, absolutely. Everyone has a personal brand—not just celebrities and sports figures, job seekers, and marketing professionals.

Think about all the ways the Internet and social media have led us to invest in some sort of a personal brand. We post, email, blog about, and text pictures of our personal life, our travels, our food, our kids, our friends, and more on all kinds of apps. What's interesting is that society's widespread understanding of a personal brand focuses on what we can see on the outside of a person's life. Branding is commonly relegated to positioning a person's external factors to look impressive on a social media post or a resume. The main problem is that an achievements-based personal brand can project what we want others to think about us, while having very little connection to the "real" us.

Photo filters exist for perfecting the selfie and transforming ourselves on screen into the epitome of living our best lives. We can hide our wrinkles and imperfections with a single click or swipe, but where is the filter for altering what's inside of us? So that we can more consistently feel better about ourselves? So that we can be sure that our life matters?

The refreshing truth is that when you're living your entire life from a place of authenticity, you recover a lot of lost energy spent filtering or masking what others can see. You no longer suffer from impostor syndrome, that gut feeling that your persona doesn't feel authentic to you or to others. Instead, you enjoy a special kind of freedom. The result is that you embrace exactly who you are—and the world finally gets to see the real you.

Your Authentic Imprint™

I call this kind of powerful personal brand Your Authentic Imprint, where you leave your unique fingerprint on the world around you. Discovering Your Authentic Imprint, learning from it, and living it out affects everything about you. My definition of personal branding is much broader than surface-level factors, like your appearance, title, or achievements. For the purpose of this book, I'd like you to consider your personal brand as Your Authentic Imprint:

> **Your Authentic Imprint is the unmistakable energy and authenticity you bring—whether in person or online—the living, breathing impression you leave on others, day after day. It's not about being more impressive, but about being more you.**

Someone asked me recently if I mainly address leaders in my coaching work, or if the principles I teach can help other people, too. The answer to both questions is yes!

I believe everyone is leading and influencing others in some way. Leadership at its core involves regularly inspiring, guiding, serving, and motivating others. While not everyone is a traditional leader (e.g., a CEO), we all have the potential to influence others at the office, at home, and in our community. Parents influence their children. Friends influence each other.

My perspective has transformed as I've witnessed profound leadership emerge from unexpected places. I've spent years not only in the corporate world but also in my local community volunteering and facilitating small groups in recovery work. What I've learned is that the most helpful definition of leaders has broader terms. In community groups, I've seen people with no formal titles or authority catalyze life-changing growth in others simply through their authenticity and willingness to be vulnerable. These experiences shattered my conventional understanding of leadership as position-based or title-dependent. Limiting leadership to organizational hierarchies misses the profound impact of what I now call "everyday leadership"— the countless moments when someone chooses to step forward, speak truth, model values, or create positive change regardless of their formal role.

Today this is how I see leaders and leadership:

**Leaders are difference makers who
want to make a positive impact.**

**Everyday Leadership is influencing positive change
through your authentic presence and purposeful actions.**

Can you see yourself in these definitions? I believe that the truths we'll explore in this book about how to lead and live from the inside out are so powerful that anyone can benefit. After all, even an executive in the most influential company goes home at the end of the workday to be a father or mother, a friend, a son or daughter, and a member of their community. Who we are is not only more important than what we do but also affects us on a daily basis.

What the Internal Revolution™ Really Means

The lifelong journey to discovering Your Authentic Imprint, learning from it, and living it out is what I call the Internal Revolution. A revolution is a disruption. Only by disrupting the way you've always done things and the way you've always lived can you start to close that gap between who you've been trying to be and the person you're called and designed to be.

Here's my definition of the Internal Revolution:

> **The Internal Revolution is the internal work necessary to rediscover your authentic strengths, lead from your core values, and reconnect with your true purpose—every single day.**

The Internal Revolution isn't about abandoning your leadership responsibilities or burning down what you've built. It's about three fundamental transformations described in this book that take place along the way in your Internal Revolution journey.

- **From Confused to Clear:** Discovering your unique strengths, values, and mission (Part 1 Live in Your Strengths)
- **From Lacking Purpose to Purposeful:** Learning to design your day (and your life) through authentic productivity (Part 2 Dominate Your Day)
- **From Isolated to Connected:** Transforming your relationships and impact through genuine presence (Part 3 Transform Your Life)

The more you know about who you really are, the easier it will be to transform from the inside out and achieve an authentic personal brand that will lead you to all the success and significance and satisfaction that you're missing. After years on my own journey toward authentic living, I've learned that true personal branding isn't about polishing your surface. It's about excavating your core. As I often say about the Internal Revolution, "Changing me changes everything."

If you have not already done so, I invite you to take the free 3-minute Authentic Imprint Assessment at danawilliamsco. scoreapp.com. It isn't required reading, but this quick tool will help you see exactly where you are now as a leader and track your transformation as you apply what you learn in this book.

Warning: an Internal Revolution is not easy. It requires sacrifice and hard work. But difference makers will do the hard work that others will not do. The benefit is that you become the leader of your own life by becoming deeply acquainted with who you are—your unique neural landscape, your authentic talents, and your true mission. The Internal Revolution is for difference makers who want to make an impact.

The Price We're Paying

The drive to constantly tweak and refine the external factors of our lives (usually for the benefit or approval of others) while ignoring who we are on the inside is costing us our sense of wellbeing in a myriad of ways. Personal and professional wellbeing are two of the most popular pursuits in modern culture, and these topics regularly find their way into top-selling books, social media feeds, and popular podcasts.

When I bring up the subject of wellbeing, everyone wants to know what to do to improve theirs—or at least have some! And no wonder. Every day there is more and more research demonstrating how detrimental the habitual stuffing down of our true selves, our true opinions, and our true desires, dreams, and goals can be. When we rest our entire identity on external factors tied to things like success, promotions, how others think of us, how well our children have "turned out" and the like, what results is a growing disconnect between body and soul.

Our external and internal selves begin to misalign, and the two grow farther apart. What begins as a few degrees off course eventually takes us far away from who we were meant to be and what we were designed to do in this life. Brand erosion describes the phenomenon when the projection of our brand (what others see) doesn't match our reality (what we know to be true about ourselves). There are warning signs of this uncomfortable dichotomy that show up in our personal and/or professional life. For example:

- Constant awareness of an authenticity gap between public image and private truth
- Others beginning to sense when you're operating from depletion
- Creeping mental and physical exhaustion of maintaining an inauthentic personal brand
- A gut feeling that things are not "right"
- Being anxious to prove something to others

This kind of personal brand management from the "outside in" saps a lot of energy from other priorities, including our health and our relationships. Leaders must take care of their own wellbeing—and watch out for that of others under their responsibility, whether serving as a team leader, or as a mom or dad. I once coached a leader who hadn't seen her elderly parents in years because she was working so hard. She hadn't taken a vacation. There was no time for personal doctor's appointments. She could never catch up and was just flat burned out. What's more, she didn't want to talk to her supervisor about it for fear that her boss would "find out I can't do it all."

Guess what? No one can do it all! The compound interest of neglecting our wellbeing cannot be overstated.

> **Your Revolution** – Think of one or two people you know who have hit the wall when it comes to their personal and/or professional wellbeing and are now suffering the consequences. What happened? Did you see it coming? What did you learn from their experience?

The Five Essential Dimensions of Wellbeing

I uncovered something transformative while leading at Southwest Airlines—a framework called the Five Essential Elements of Wellbeing by Gallup, a global analytics and advisory firm known for its workplace research and strengths-based development. Gallup has conducted extensive research in the context of Wellbeing in over 150 countries encompassing over 98% of the world's population. They discovered Wellbeing is multi-dimensional and includes certain critical areas of our lives that yield a well-rounded picture. Gallup identified five universal and interrelated elements of Wellbeing, with each dimension representing a distinct facet of life that we can influence and improve:[1] When the following five elements are in balance, Wellbeing emerges naturally:

1. Career Wellbeing – Liking what you do each day*
*I broaden Career Wellbeing to include having a "Purpose"

According to Gallup, this is the most powerful predictor of overall life satisfaction. It is about how you occupy your time, whether through work or other meaningful activities, and it is considered the foundation for the other elements.[2] Gallup's research shows that people with high Wellbeing in this area are more likely to be engaged, miss less work due to poor health, and report greater overall life satisfaction.[3] People are also more than twice as likely to be thriving in their lives overall and significantly less likely to experience anxiety, worry, and stress—all elements of Wellbeing that emerge naturally when we engage in meaningful work.

Purpose is woven into our chosen career or calling (for those who work outside the office). If we are regularly neglecting our life's greater purpose, we may experience things like:

- A sense of disconnection from what matters most
- Diminished creativity
- Difficulty in decision-making
- Lack of presence—you're there, but a million miles away

2. Social Wellbeing – Maintaining meaningful relationships

Dr. Vivek Murthy, former U.S. Surgeon General, has long advocated that loneliness represents a public health crisis comparable to smoking or obesity. Gallup's research shows that Social Wellbeing isn't just about having relationships but about having relationships where you can be your authentic self. This includes friendships, family, and social connections that provide positive energy and encouragement.[4] Their studies also reveal that having at least six hours of social interaction daily (either through in-person conversations, phone calls, or digital communication) significantly increases Wellbeing.

Supportive social relationships are critical for emotional resilience and daily happiness. Neglecting our Wellbeing often shows up this way:

- Lack of enjoyment of relationships
- Difficulty setting boundaries with others
- Habitual people-pleasing
- Co-dependency

3. Financial Wellbeing – Having enough of what you need

Financial Wellbeing is about having the security, resources, and perspective to support the life you uniquely want to live. It's about effectively managing your economic life to reduce stress and increase security. It is not just about income but also about feeling secure and in control of your finances.[5] People with high Financial Wellbeing experience less stress and are more able to pursue their goals and interests.

Financially neglecting ourselves may also lead to negative consequences. Let's face it. Managing a personal brand strictly from an external point of view can get expensive from a purely practical perspective. It costs money to put our energy into securing the "right" education and landing the "right" job. The same is true for impressing the "right" people in our circles—spending whatever it takes to look the part, from what we wear to work or at community functions, or what we drive in the carpool line at school.

I recently worked with James, a highly compensated executive experiencing constant financial stress, despite his objectively comfortable position. Through our sessions, he discovered his relationship with money was being driven by subconscious patterns formed during childhood financial insecurity—creating a cycle where no amount ever felt "enough."

By bringing these patterns into awareness and aligning his spending with his core values rather than unconscious fears, James created both financial security and emotional freedom. "I realized I was trying to solve an emotional problem with financial solutions," he shared. "Now I make decisions from clarity instead of anxiety."

4. Physical Wellbeing – Honoring Your Unique Needs in a Productivity-Obsessed Culture

Neglecting ourselves often shows up very clearly in our physical body. Dan Buettner's groundbreaking research with the world's "Blue Zones"—regions with the highest concentration of centenarians—offers profound insights into sustainable physical health that challenge our conventional wisdom. As a National Geographic researcher, Buettner discovered that the world's longest-lived people don't follow intense exercise regimens but instead integrate natural movement into their daily lives. Rather than approaching physical wellbeing through intense but unsustainable interventions, Blue Zone residents maintain consistent, modest habits that align with their natural rhythms. Buettner's research and personal practice show that physical vitality emerges more from aligned daily habits than from fighting against our natural patterns.

Physical Wellbeing refers to having good health and enough energy to get things done on a daily basis. It encompasses exercise, nutrition, sleep, and overall physical health.[6] High Physical Wellbeing is linked to greater productivity, less absenteeism at work, and a higher likelihood of recovering from illness or hardship.[7]

The tell-tale physical signs of not paying enough attention in this area include:

- Weight gain (or loss)
- Stress eating (or not eating)
- Sleeplessness (or the desire to sleep more than necessary)
- Chronic stress
- Energy depletion
- Worry and anxiety

5. Community Wellbeing – Belonging and Giving Back

Community Wellbeing is the sense of engagement with and contribution to the places and groups where you live and work. For example: volunteer commitments, neighborhood gatherings, or professional group participation.

Gallup research shows that people with high Community Wellbeing display greater emotional resilience. Involvement in a community serves as a buffer against stress and isolation and involves a sense of engagement and pride associated with where you live. It includes liking where you live, feeling safe, and having opportunities to contribute to your community.[8] When we ignore this area, we risk:

- Lacking an effective outlet for stress at home and/or work
- Missing opportunities to bond with our spouse, family members, or friends to serve together
- Over-committing to depleting meetings, functions, etc.
- Anxiety resulting from not feeling safe or connected to where we live

José Andrés' journey from acclaimed chef to humanitarian leader perfectly illustrates how authentic contribution emerges when we apply our unique talents to community needs. As a world-renowned chef, Andrés found deeper purpose through founding World Central Kitchen, which serves meals in disaster zones worldwide. What began as a response to the 2010 Haiti earthquake has grown into a global organization that has served over 70 million meals. His story demonstrates how bringing your existing skills to community needs—rather than attempting to contribute in ways misaligned with your strengths—creates sustainable impact that enhances yourself in the process.

How I Track Wellbeing

I realized how vital it was to stay on top of these key areas, but I could not find an easy way to measure them weekly. I created The Strengths Journal™—the only Gallup-certified licensed daily planner. The Weekly Scorecard is one feature in the journal. It's simple, but powerful, and holds me accountable to an honest evaluation of these five areas of Wellbeing at the end of every week. I simply assign a number reflecting how well I did the previous week in each area: (1-poor; 5=excellent).

For example, this weekly practice helps me see that I may have a handle on my physical health one week, but it's been a long time since I've prioritized being with my girlfriends who build me up and encourage me. Sometimes you may have your finances in a row, but at the same time your health is going off the rails. Regular evaluation of these areas helps us learn to spot some of the classic outward manifestations that signal we've neglected one or more of these categories.

The Weekly Scorecard is just one of the powerful habits I use every day as part of my Internal Revolution. "Daily" is how the Internal Revolution takes place. Daily practice has transformed my business and my life more than anything else. It's that influential. We'll explore more of the incredible compounding power of consistent daily transformation in Part 2 Dominate Your Day.

Life as an Investment

Think of your life as an investment strategy. Many people put 90% of their energy into nurturing ourselves in one area, while neglecting critical diversification across the other areas that contribute to our inner sense of peace and vitality. For some, that 90% goes to their professional achievements. For others, that 90% may go to working out or obsessing about money. An investment heavily weighted to one dimension, to the neglect of caring for all other areas, is lopsided.

Another visual is of an iceberg floating in the Arctic. What others see is our impressive visible success—at work, at school, in the community, with our family—but the hidden costs of maintaining our success to the neglect of other things are all lurking below the surface.

In fact, Gallup has concluded only about 7% of people globally are thriving in all five areas of Wellbeing, highlighting the challenge all the more.[9] The contradiction between how we truly want to live and how we're actually living are all too familiar to many people. We're disconnected from ourselves, while at the same time trying to lead others. This is as true in the business arena as it is when we're unbalanced and trying to help lead our families, impact our community, and maintain healthy personal relationships.

In contrast to all this frenetic external juggling of appearances, the Internal Revolution of building Your Authentic Imprint begins exactly where you might expect—on the inside. I wrote this book out of the conviction that everyone can benefit from an Internal Revolution. We need to focus more of our daily energy on the greater internal work that must be done in order to present who we really are to the world—confidently and whole-heartedly—and fulfill our own unique destiny to the hilt. No one else is called to do what you alone can accomplish in this life. As Oscar Wilde once quipped, "Be yourself. Everyone else is taken."

The goal is to introduce you to life-changing principles that help you take specific action, get back on track, and live more authentically. Instead of teaching you how to create the perfect Instagram profile or how to refine your elevator pitch in the marketplace, we're going on a deep dive inside to build your brand from the inside out.

The human heart is a fertile field and unplowed ground for developing Your Authentic Imprint and coming to terms with who we were designed to be, what we are uniquely destined to accomplish, and how to best go about pursuing that purpose for the rest of our lives.

Four Strategies to Jumpstart Your Internal Revolution

In these first few chapters of Part I Live in Your Strengths, we're laying a crucial foundation for your Internal Revolution so that it has real staying power. I'll show you how to implement four strategies of Your Authentic Imprint (and understand how they work together) to transform your life and also multiply your impact on the world around you. I put these four strategies together in an easy-to-use formula for intentional daily living that produces Your Authentic Imprint:

(Strengths + Core Values + Mission) × Emotional Recognition = Your Authentic Imprint

Think about this formula as the shot heard 'round the world heralding the beginning of your Internal Revolution. We'll unpack these four strategies represented in this formula in the next few chapters, but here is an overview of each one to get you thinking:

Strategy 1: Gain a general understanding of your strengths and talents

In addition to Wellbeing research, Gallup is perhaps best known for creating an assessment called CliftonStrengths (previously StrengthsFinder). Over 35 million people have taken the assessment to identify their natural patterns of thinking, feeling, and behaving. Although you do not have to take this assessment to find your strengths or benefit from this book, I recommend doing so because it will provide in-depth insights regarding your particular strengths. Find more information on CliftonStrengths at www.danawilliamsco.com/code.

I took the CliftonStrengths Assessment while leading at Southwest Airlines and discovered my top strengths included what Gallup terms Ideation, Futuristic, and Maximizer. I have a natural ability to and generate innovative ideas (Ideation), envision and strategize about the future (Futuristic), and prioritize excellence in my work (Maximizer). It didn't just give me words to describe my talents. These insights gave me access to an internal power source I didn't know I had.

When old habits of scarcity thinking would creep in, I learned to use my strengths to see possibilities I'd never noticed before. It was as if I'd discovered how to plug into an energy source that had been there all along, waiting to be uncovered.

This revelation regarding how our brains are uniquely wired for certain talents became so central to my understanding of authentic living and leadership that I decided to become a Gallup-certified CliftonStrengths coach so I could show others how to live in their strengths. I also helped Southwest Airlines become the first strengths-based airline.

Eventually, I built the leadership consulting business I have today guiding thousands of business leaders and others from burnout to breakthrough by living and leading in their strengths. I've discovered that sustainable transformation begins with a dual investment: first in understanding your natural wiring, then in applying your strengths to elevate your entire life.

Strategy 2: Identifying Your Core Values
We know parts of what self-discovery looks like and what it means innately. When we "speak from the heart," for example, we come the closest to tapping into the person we really are.

What do we mean when we say that? We mean that we are speaking from a place deep inside of us that is intimate and wholly alive and real. Our decisions come more easily, and our words are authentic and true when they arise from our core values—those non-negotiables regarding what is most important to us. Do you know your core values and how they may have changed over time? Are you operating out of them day-to-day? They form the foundation of your personal brand.

Strategy 3: Learn to Live Out Your Mission
When you leverage your natural talents in service of a greater purpose for living, you transform ordinary leadership moments into meaningful impact. That's your mission. How do others experience and benefit from you living your purpose—or how could they? When you pursue your mission and align your daily actions with purpose, you may not realize that you're also creating a beacon for others to follow.

Strategy 4: Multiply Your Efforts by Practicing Emotional Recognition
What is emotional recognition? Here's a definition: **Emotional recognition is the ability to notice, name, and understand your emotional state before it shapes your actions or relationships.** Notice the multiplication sign in the

formula. Emotional recognition multiplies the impact of our strengths, core values, and mission—especially during times of change—in our daily lives. Emotional recognition isn't just another add-on; it's what transforms your internal awareness into visible leadership during times of change.

How we manage ourselves—our thoughts, reactions, and choices—forms the foundation of our daily Internal Revolution. It's never one and done. Each day presents new opportunities to either react from old patterns or respond from our authentic core. Your journey of discovery is uniquely yours. Some practices you'll learn in this book might resonate deeply, while other exercises will challenge you. That's part of the process. The key is to engage with each one openly, allowing yourself to discover what lies beneath.

A Collapse That Led to Self-Discovery

I'm passionate about helping others live out their Authentic Imprint because I'm writing out of lived experience. Like many people, I spent years as a professional people-pleaser and self-appointed fixer of others. I thought I was building stability, but really, I was constructing elaborate facades. By the time I'd become an expert at managing everyone else's life, I had lost touch with my own.

In 2008, my own carefully constructed world began to crumble. As the economy collapsed on a global stage, my personal world followed suit. I was looking at a twenty-five-year marriage in crisis, financial devastation, and my husband's prostate cancer diagnosis. Our only daughter was away at college, and I found myself alone amid the ruins of everything I once thought defined me. What seemed as if it were the end turned out to be a new beginning.

After clocking many miles on the journey of self-discovery and after a number of years of recovering from the destruction of all that was familiar to me, I looked back at how far I'd come. In short, our marriage had been fully restored through years of intentional work, my husband was cancer-free and in recovery, and we were ready for a new adventure together. We had the opportunity to visit Egypt, a country that draws archeologists and researchers from all over the globe because of the glittery promise of the next discovery. Copious amounts of desert sand are chock full of ancient artifacts perfectly preserved in the arid climate. From the pyramids of Giza to the Valley of the Kings and Saqqara, the entire region is a constantly ongoing archeological dig.

Standing before the incredible wonders of the Great Pyramids, our tour guide explained that the reason these giant pyramids are still standing today is because they were built on a limestone plateau that keeps the pyramids from sinking into the surrounding desert sands. It was so clear to me in that moment that the facades, the protective walls, and the carefully constructed external images we build on shifting sand in our lives eventually break down. All that can withstand the passing of time must be built a true foundation, unseen but unshakeable. For me, that foundation begins by knowing God, my ultimate source of strength and wisdom.

Then the tour guide explained that the most amazing insight

about these icons was something we could not see from our vantage point at the base of the pyramids. He pointed out that these ancient structures contain multi-story hidden chambers inside that house innumerable sacred artifacts. I marveled at the architectural paradox that reflected my own journey of personal transformation. One step at a time, I was building a testament to human perseverance and possibility—on the inside.

The Egyptians cleverly built their monuments from the inside out over a period of twenty years, carefully placing each stone to create something that would last millennia and protect their most valuable treasures. Likewise, I was struck by the fact that each of us carries layers of undiscovered treasures within— our experiences, values, beliefs—that even the people who are closest to us have never seen. Our authentic selves require the same careful excavation and patient uncovering of what lies beneath that archeologists give to discovering what's been hiding for thousands of years inside the pyramids.

My husband and I found ourselves on yet another journey of discovery later on in our trip—this time on a sunrise hike up Mount Sinai on the Sinai Peninsula. At 2:00 AM, our group of nine began the ascent in complete darkness, equipped with flashlights, climbing shoes, and warm clothing. It wasn't lost on me that Moses had made this climb eight times in simple sandals while we were struggling despite our modern gear! In the darkness we could only see a few feet ahead on the trail, and I often wondered if we'd ever reach the destination. As we walked onward for hours, the thin air and rocky terrain demanded complete focus.

What struck me most about the Mt. Sinai climb happened just as we reached the summit. We were among the few

Americans there, surrounded by people from Russia, Germany, France, China, and many other nations. All gathered in the pre-dawn darkness, all awaiting the same revelation promised at sunrise. Some sang, others prayed. But all of us connected in our shared journey toward something greater than ourselves.

Personal growth often requires taking the next step without seeing the entire path, and nothing takes more concentrated work over long periods of time than internal change. But the rewards along the way are invaluable, like my photos from the summit of Mt. Sinai that morning.

Draw Your Life Map: Your Story So Far

A wise counselor introduced me to what remains one of my most valuable tools to this day: the Life Map. He explained that before we can choose a new direction, we need to understand the path that brought us to this point. The simple exercise I learned involved drawing out my life's journey so far on paper. I did this exercise early in my personal transformation, and I saw patterns in my life that I'd never noticed before. For example, I began to see connections between my father's anxiety about money and my own need for control, between my mother's work habits and my tendency to escape through busyness.

To start your own Life Map, take a sheet of paper and draw a horizontal line. Label the left end of the line "Birth" and the right end of the line "Today." On this timeline, mark significant events—both high and low points—that have occurred so far in your life.

As you step back and think about the events on your Life Map, reflect on these questions:

- What patterns do you notice? What beliefs, habits, or coping mechanisms did you pick up from parents, teachers, or other influencers?
- Which patterns have you carried forward—both those that serve you and those that hinder you?
- Are you holding onto anger, resentment, people-pleasing, or other habits that no longer fit who you are or want to be?
- Is there anyone—others, yourself, or even God—you need to forgive?

The Life Map helps you make friends with the hard things in your life. When circumstances are difficult, we often carry shame regarding those situations. Somehow, that dark shame begins to dissolve when we map it and bring it into the light.

Be willing to look at what's difficult—those things you might not want to face but need to examine so that growth can take place. The Life Map helps you make peace with the challenging parts of your past as you plan your path forward. It's not about judging or criticizing your past experiences; it's about understanding the patterns in your life and making intentional choices about how to move forward.

We're not meant to do this work alone, by the way. I invite you to do this Life Map exercise with an accountability partner or a licensed professional counselor if you choose. I'm not a professional counselor—just someone who did my own internal work with an accountability partner as well as a wise professional counselor and saw deep inner change as a result. As you'll read about in a later chapter, I took decisive action on what I uncovered in my Life Map, and that has made all the difference.

Looking Ahead

In Chapter 2, we'll build upon these initial discoveries and explore the first component of the formula for intentional daily living—how to find your strengths. We'll look at how your unique neural wiring can transform how you navigate both challenges and opportunities. You'll begin to understand just how remarkable this internal wiring really is and how your unique circuitry shows up in the form of strengths that are designed for specific purposes. One of the greatest discoveries you'll ever make is the power grid that's already installed within you. Learning to manage energy, versus time management, is one of the most life-changing skills you'll ever apply.

Worth Remembering

Revolution happens one choice at a time. Start small, stay consistent, trust the process. Your foundation comes from God, unseen but unshakeable. The work of managing your internal world happens daily.

PUTTING IT INTO PRACTICE

QUESTIONS FOR REFLECTION

1. What patterns in your life feel ready for change?
2. Where do you sense God's hand or a power outside of yourself at work in your story?
3. Who helps you stay grounded in your authentic self?
4. What small, daily practice in one of the five areas of Wellbeing feels both doable and meaningful?

EXERCISE 1
YOUR PATTERN RECOGNITION MOMENT

Throughout our journey across Egypt, an Egyptologist interpreted the hieroglyphics at various ancient sites. Each hieroglyph held deeper meaning beyond the symbols on a wall. Likewise, our own lives contain patterns and messages waiting to be decoded. These ancient Egyptians had recorded their stories, beliefs, and transformations in stone; we carry ours within, waiting to be told.

This week, call on an accountability partner—someone you trust and who is always helping you be your best. Tell him or her three stories about recent challenges you've had. Look for common threads as you objectively listen to yourself recount the circumstances. You might discover patterns you never noticed before about how you approach and handle problems. For example:

- Do you use language that makes you sound like a victim of your circumstances?
- Do you catch yourself using controlling language?
- Are you overly negative or critical?
- Do you come across as co-dependent, trying to take care of everyone except yourself?
- What personal strengths come across in talking about your challenges?

EXERCISE 2
STRENGTHS SPOTTING

Notice throughout your day when you feel most energized doing certain tasks and fulfilling specific responsibilities.

- Reflect on your calendar from the last two weeks and draw a circle around those things you feel you could naturally do for hours without interruption. Draw a square around things that "box you in" and drain your energy.
- What natural talents and skillsets are you using in those energetic moments? These are initial clues to your authentic strengths.

EXERCISE 3
DAILY EVALUATION

Choose one of the simple evaluation questions below to ask yourself throughout the day whenever you feel stuck or frustrated. For example:

What's mine to manage? (Can help identify control issues.)

What am I doing that I should stop doing? (Can help identify boundaries issues.)

What do I need to start doing instead? (Can help identify procrastination issues.)

You might use different evaluation questions. The key is making the questions simple enough to remember, profound enough to matter.

Scan to take the free Authentic Imprint Assessment to see where you are on your journey.

danawilliamsco.scoreapp.com

CHAPTER 2

Discovering Your Strengths: Tapping into Your Internal Power Grid

Singapore is one of the most energy-efficient countries on earth, with power disruption estimated at less than one minute per customer per year. That's impressive, but the world's most sophisticated natural power grid is the one housed inside of you. Just like a city's electrical system, your brain has high-capacity transmission lines designed to carry massive amounts of energy to power your activities every day.

These transmission lines are your natural talents—those recurring patterns of thoughts, feelings, and behaviors that make you "you," as well as the energy-producing areas of strength that you naturally gravitate toward. You started identifying your core strengths in the previous chapter, so now it's time to put them in the context of Your Authentic Imprint formula for intentional daily living:

$$(\text{Strengths} + \text{Core Values} + \text{Mission}) \times \text{Emotional Recognition} = \text{Your Authentic Imprint}$$

Some of you may already have a good idea of some of your strengths. You may not be able to put a name on all of the things you are "good at," but it's likely that people have told you throughout life that you have this or that natural affinity, talent, or strength.

Your strengths develop over time as you acquire certain skills, knowledge, and lived experience. Identifying and operating from your top strengths—typically three and up to five—is crucial to effective energy management and an overall sense of wellbeing. Strengths is the first element in the formula because they take you along the shortest path to living out Your Authentic Imprint.

Sometimes people are surprised to realize that they indeed have a certain strength. Either they haven't exercised that strength much—or they have been unfairly convinced by someone (or some circumstances) that they cannot succeed in that area. So they don't try. That is just another symptom of not really being in touch with who we are designed to be. However, when you decide to grow and begin to tap into Your Authentic Imprint, you have the chance to summon your courage and try all that was once improbable and seemingly impossible.

What Are Your Strengths?

Building on the simple Strengths Spotting exercise you did in Chapter 1, think through your answers to the following questions regarding what you do best.

1. **What energizes you?** What activities make you lose track of time?
2. **What do people ask you for help with?** In what ways do friends, family, and colleagues naturally come to you for help?
3. **What feels effortless?** What do others say is "hard" but feels easy to you?
4. **What patterns do you see?** Looking back at your wins, what was your unique contribution?
5. **What would a stranger understand about what you do naturally just by observing you?** In answer to that question, I've often heard people describe their strengths this way:
    * "Seeing solutions others miss"
    * "Making people feel heard and understood"
    * "Getting things done that others struggle with"
    * "Connecting ideas in new ways"
    * "Bringing out the best in people"
    * "Simplifying the complicated"

Four Strengths Domains

All of us have many diverse strengths, and these strengths generally fall into four recognizable categories or domains. CliftonStrengths describes the four domains this way:

Executing – Strengths that help you get things done
Influencing – Strengths that help you lead and persuade others
Relationship Building – Strengths that help you build strong
relationships
Strategic Thinking – Strengths that help you organize and plan

In my coaching sessions, I reference these four domains to help clients connect with their unique strengths. By answering some simple questions in these four categories, people can naturally identify several of their top strengths.

1. **Executing** – Strengths that help you get things done
   - How important is structure and organization in your daily life?
   - What's your approach to meeting deadlines and commitments?
   - Do you prefer having clear instructions or figuring things out yourself?

2. **Influencing** – Strengths that help you lead and persuade others
   - How often have you successfully convinced others to support your ideas?
   - How comfortable are you taking charge in uncertain situations?
   - In what contexts do you naturally speak up or take the lead?

3. **Relationship Building** – Strengths that help you build strong relationships

- How do you typically respond when someone shares something difficult with you?
- In what situations do you find yourself connecting people or ideas?
- What roles do you tend to take in group settings?

4. **Strategic Thinking** – Strengths that help you organize and plan
   - How do you approach complex problems?
   - Do you often think about future possibilities or scenarios?
   - What types of information do you naturally collect or remember?

Which of the four domains holds the most resonant answers for you? That category likely contains many of your natural talents. What specific strengths feel most natural to you? (Example: "I naturally organize information" or "I instinctively build deep relationships.")

Can you now name three to five strengths you've spotted so far, based on these four domains, as well as your answers to the corresponding reflective questions? Knowing and using your strengths enhances your internal life and increases the external impact you have, whether the team you're responsible for at work or the friends and family members in your life. Identifying your strengths is like unwrapping a gift to yourself. Using your particular strengths more intentionally is like giving a gift to the world.

Connect Your Strengths to Wellbeing

Difference makers realize that operating more and more from one's strengths is the secret to making a lasting impact that doesn't burn you out. Operating day to day in your unique strengths supercharges how you feel about yourself and how you're presenting yourself to the world as you learn to live out Your Authentic Imprint. Instead of being exhausted at the end of a day, you're surprisingly energized.

Now think about the close relationship between your top strengths and the five dimensions of Wellbeing you learned in chapter 1. For example:

1. If you enjoy creating structure and order (Executing), consider how this strength might enhance your Physical Wellbeing by helping you establish consistent health routines that feel natural rather than forced.
2. If you're naturally good at building connections (Relationship Building), your Social Wellbeing might be energized by using that strength in meaningful one-on-one conversations or going to networking/community events.
3. If you excel at thinking about future possibilities (Strategic Thinking), that strength can boost your Career Wellbeing (having a Purpose) by dedicating regular time to envision your personal and professional growth, rather than focusing solely on just day-to-day tasks.
4. If you naturally take charge in group settings (Influencing), your Community Wellbeing will flourish if you use those strengths to steer a community activity you enjoy. For example, you might prefer leading a rally

to raise money for cancer research rather than participating passively (e.g., sitting behind a table at a community wide garage sale).

How do your strengths shape how others see you? Which strengths would you like to be more known for? Recall our definition: **Your Authentic Imprint is the unmistakable energy and authenticity you bring—whether in person or online—the living, breathing impression you leave on others, day after day. It's not about being more impressive, but about being more you.** Strengths can be viewed as energy sources and amplifiers of what we know to be true about ourselves. By understanding and applying your natural strengths daily, you create alignment between your wellbeing and the authentic brand you present to the world—transforming both in the process.

> **Your Revolution** – When was the first time you realized you had a natural talent and affinity in a certain area? What was that like? How did that discovery lead to other opportunities in your life down the road?

Understanding Your Unique Circuitry

Your brain's power grid is incredibly complex. Scientists have discovered that the brain contains roughly 86 billion neurons, each capable of forming up to 15,000 connections with other neurons. Our Milky Way galaxy alone contains 100-400 billion stars, but our neural network is more expansive than all the stars in multiple galaxies combined!

If each neural connection in your brain was a light bulb in our power grid metaphor, you'd have enough lights to illuminate thousands of cities. And just like every city has its unique pattern of lights when viewed from space, your neural pattern is uniquely yours.

How unique? According to Gallup's research, the probability of someone sharing your exact sequence of top five strengths is 1 in 33 million. Living in Texas, I'd have to gather the entire state's population of 28 million people, then find 5 million more people outside our borders just to find one other person with the same combination of talents, in the same order, as me. Even then, they would use those talents differently because of their unique experiences and neural pathways.

Understanding your internal power grid is one thing; learning to live through it intentionally is another. Just as a city's power grid requires constant monitoring and adjustment, your internal grid needs daily attention and intentional direction. Think about it. Power plant managers don't just understand how electricity works. They actively monitor flow, adjust for peak usage times, and perform regular maintenance. Similarly, managing your internal power grid isn't just about knowing your strengths. It's about intentionally directing your energy through internal high-capacity lines each day.

Here's a crucial truth I've learned: managing yourself through your strengths isn't about managing your time; it's about managing your energy. When you're working through your natural talents, you'll find yourself energized rather than drained, even after tackling challenging tasks. Let's identify some common energy zappers in order to avoid blowing a fuse.

Energy Zapper: Operating outside of your strengths too much and too often

Let me begin with a cautionary tale. In your home, you cannot force too much electrical current through smaller circuits or disaster strikes. Best case, whatever you're trying to power up may run extra slow, like a European hair dryer that never gets hot enough in the USA because of the voltage difference between the two countries. If you or your spouse have ever plugged in your hair dryer overseas without a power converter, you have an instant visual! What happens? Burnout and complete shutdown.

Yet this is exactly what we do when we spend our days working against our natural wiring, instead of living and working in our own unique strengths and enjoying the natural flow of energy day to day. I see this low-energy-flow and eventual burnout frequently among individuals and in whole companies.

In the business world, some leaders try to copy others' management styles instead of leading authentically through their strengths. One executive I worked with was draining herself trying to be the charismatic, extroverted leader she thought her team needed. When she discovered that her natural talents were more along the lines of strategic thinking and helping team members one-on-one, everything shifted. Instead of performing exhausting theatrical presentations in team meetings, she instead began leading through thoughtful one-on-one conversations and innovative problem-solving. This conscious pivot energized both herself and her team, and it was easier to accomplish because she was living authentically as the leader she is, not the leader she was trying to be.

When we take on too much, requiring skills and strengths

we don't have, it's akin to trying to power a whole neighborhood through a single household line. It can't be done! Your brain has smaller circuits that can handle some power but aren't built for heavy loads. These smaller circuits are the abilities you've developed but they aren't your core strengths. Everyone has to do things they don't like (and aren't necessarily good at doing) from time to time. There are parts of every job description that challenge us to work outside of our strengths. Likewise, there are elements of our family and household responsibilities that do the same. That's life. However, the goal is to structure your day (and your life) so that you do more of what you're built to do, and less of the other.

Get a Daily and Weekly System

To help people harness this energy daily, I encourage using a tool like The Strengths Journal, which can also serve as a companion guide to CliftonStrengths. I personally use it every day as a guide for channeling my limited daily energy through my natural power lines. The daily habit of journaling offers a structured way to engage and direct your energy intentionally each day toward those things that matter most.

Here's what I appreciate about having a system like The Strengths Journal to guide me so I can live with purpose every day:

- **It doesn't take long.** The Strengths Journal is one page per day that I can complete in less than 7 minutes.
- **It focuses me.** I define my desired outcome for the day and why I want that result.

- **It helps me take action.** I typically list up to three actions I can take toward my desired outcome—and I match those actions with a personal strength I can use to ensure success.

That's what I do daily. In addition, I do a weekly review and chart ahead some of my goals for the next week. The Strengths Journal system also helps me accomplish a weekly evaluation so I can:

- **See patterns of where my energy is going.** I note when I was most energized in a particular task.
- **Set myself up for success for next week.** I start shaping my upcoming goals ahead of time.
- **Map brave steps that honor my authentic leadership.** I identify specific actions that align with my unique talents, steadily moving through fear and confidence gaps toward my goals.

Whether you use The Strengths Journal or create your own system, the key is daily practice aligning your energy with your natural talents. Creating consistent good habits is one way to rewire your subconscious, like an electrician replacing all the old burned-out wiring (bad habits) with new wiring. Each day you can power up good habits based on your unique talents.

There are certain habits and routines that are almost certain to blow a fuse in our attempts to manage our energy better. I call these Energy Zappers. When you plug into those bad habits, that old wiring drains your inner strength. Take caution and look out for these—they can destroy the precious energy you'll need to be successful in your Internal Revolution.

Energy Zapper: Falling into the trap of scarcity thinking

Scarcity thinking happens when we focus heavily on what we lack, whether that's resources, time, and/or opportunities. This mindset isn't just about having limited resources; it's about how that limitation affects our thinking and decisions. [10] Like a power grid operating at minimum capacity, scarcity thinking reduces our mental bandwidth and can lead to further limitations, especially when life throws us curveballs.

It's not surprising that research shows that only 3% of people are living the way they truly want to live. The rest? They're going after things they already know how to get—the safe choices, the popular decisions, the paths that require no courage. That's limited, scarcity thinking. But people don't become difference makers by playing it safe. They create lasting impact by making decisions that signal growth and abundance and align with their authentic selves, even when those decisions feel uncomfortable.

Take the senior leader I recently coached—someone with incredible relationship and strategic thinking talents. "I know I'm people-pleasing this situation," he told me, "and I just need to move forward." His awareness was the first step before he could learn to leverage his strengths to make the decision his organization desperately needed.

As I mentioned earlier, my father's constant anxiety about money shaped my early understanding of resources and possibility. His scarcity mindset wasn't just about finances; it colored how he viewed everything, from opportunities to relationships. Because I inherited his same lens through which to see the world, I'm vulnerable to unconsciously viewing life through the filter of "not enough." Learning to operate from a perspective of abundance instead of scarcity has been a deep focus for me, especially while running my own business.

Energy Zapper: Unhealthy fear

Fear itself is not the enemy. The problem is not knowing how to direct energy to our strengths in order to defeat the unhealthy kind of fear. There is a difference between healthy and unhealthy fear. Healthy fear serves as a survival mechanism—it's a built-in power surge protector that throws a switch when we get ourselves in potentially dangerous situations. For example, fear of pain teaches us as a child not to touch a hot stove. Fear of strangers keeps us safe on the street.

However, the Hebrew word for fear (phobos) describes detrimental fear, and it's where we get our English word "phobia." This type of unhealthy fear overloads the circuits by being disproportionate to the actual danger. For example, we often overestimate threats and underestimate our ability to cope. We come across a challenging situation and our strengths go out the window!

I've experienced firsthand how unhealthy fear can direct energy away from our natural strengths and render us seemingly powerless. When I was planning my wedding at the young age of 20, I became convinced that it would snow on my wedding day. It wasn't unheard of to have ice storms in January in Dallas, and I spent months worrying about the potential for a blizzard. "I hope it doesn't snow" became my mantra amid every wedding conversation. Instead of using my Futuristic strength to envision positive possibilities, I caved to my fears.

In a classic case of self-fulfilling prophecy, we experienced one of the worst ice storms in Dallas history that January! I mean, seven days of ice, no power, and closed roads! Thankfully, the power came back on just in time, the wedding went off without a hitch, and over 40 years later that storm is just part of our story. How much energy I wasted instead of combating fear with my inner strength.

Just as a city's power grid needs a reliable power source, our internal grid requires connection to an ultimate power source. For me, that's God. But that wasn't always the case. I discovered this truth gradually. Years of recovery work revealed something transformative—God does not want us to live in negative, unhealthy fear. It's no coincidence that "Do not be afraid" is one of the most frequent commands in the Bible. But it does talk about the "fear of God." What does that mean? It doesn't mean to be afraid of God. Healthy fear simply means awe, respect, and the recognition of God's omniscience, majesty, and holiness. That kind of fear is the antidote to all other fears. When we truly fear and revere an almighty God, what else is there to fear in life?

Energy Zapper: Stretching yourself too thin

Erin Duncan's journey of transformation and leadership is nothing short of inspirational. Today, Erin is a strategic advisor who coaches individuals and teams to develop and execute strategies with clarity and speed through the power of purposeful decision-making. But first she had to learn how to live her life by design and not by default.

Nearly five years ago, Erin stepped into a position demanding a complete overhaul of team structures and processes. It was a challenge tailor-made for someone like her, who thrives on solving complex problems and driving impactful changes. However, this role demanded more than just professional commitment; it required sacrificing her personal time and cut into her wellbeing.

As Erin immersed herself in her work, the consequence of neglecting other aspects of her life began to manifest in physical ways. Despite excelling in her career, she suffered from chronic pain and rising blood pressure—clear indicators that something was amiss. Energy was seeping out of her with no replenishment.

It was a conversation with a close friend and member of her virtual "board of directors" (more on that later) that became a wake-up call. He urged Erin to rethink her unsustainable lifestyle. As leaders, difference makers, moms, dads, visionaries, and entrepreneurs, we often naively believe we can do it all. But Erin's story challenges this notion, emphasizing the importance of understanding our limited energy stores and instead pursuing holistic wellbeing in our journeys.

Her transformation began with recognizing the need for boundaries and seeking professional help to address underlying issues. She also revisited her life strategy, aligning her energy and daily actions with her long-term goals. One particularly striking aspect of Erin's narrative is how she used her unique strengths to navigate her transformation. These qualities helped her envision a future where she could balance success with satisfaction without compromising her health.

This leader's journey is a powerful reminder that success shouldn't come at the cost of our health or happiness. Managing our energy is essential. As we continue to push through our limits at times and chase what we want out of life, let's not forget to measure our wellbeing, set boundaries, and listen to our bodies.

Erin's story is not just about transformation, however. It's about realization and reorientation to Your Authentic Imprint. Today Erin is someone who values her wellbeing as much as her achievements. She shows that it's possible to redesign our lives around our true priorities and emerge energized, healthier, and more fulfilled.

Energy Zapper: Relying on yourself alone for power

Successful people learn to manage their energy by tapping into a reservoir of power outside of themselves. I hardly ever start my day without quiet time connecting to my divine power source. I journal, study, or I'm simply being still in God's presence. I've learned to ask for spiritual eyes to see and spiritual ears to hear what God needs me to know and do each day. It's not about relying on my own power but staying plugged into an infinite source of strength.

Through this connection to my power source, I find I can listen to God, rather than the overbearing noise of our culture and my own distracting thoughts. I have better focus on my God-given talents, rather than a narrow or limiting obsession with what others want me to do with my life. I learn to direct my energy through my natural strengths in these moments. And I have more control over my thoughts because I ask God to help me.

Growing up, my relationship with God was more about

appearances than connection: attending church, participating in activities, being "a good girl." It wasn't until my early twenties that I realized something vital was missing. Through the guidance of a pastor who invested in my husband and me through Bible studies, I began to understand what it means to have a genuine relationship with God.

The more I learned about the Bible and developed this relationship, the more I craved that divine connection. I discovered that starting my day with God (whether through devotionals, Bible study, or simply journaling my conversations with God) grounded me in a way nothing else could do. This practice became my power source and was especially crucial when my life and marriage hit rock bottom years later. Because I had filled myself with the truth about God, I had a reservoir of strength to draw from during those challenging times.

The point is to avoid relying only on yourself for the power you need in life. That's a major energy zapper because human power is limited. The alternative is to have a ready and daily connection to a source greater than yourself, especially when you feel run down and drained. When we're plugged into a divine or "other" power source, our natural talents become channels for purpose and impact. The question isn't whether you have power available. It's available to you. The issue is whether you're connected to the source and are allowing energy to flow through your natural pathways to overcome any challenge.

Your power grid is divinely designed for you. You don't need to replicate someone else's circuitry—just start maximizing the flow through your own high-capacity power lines.

Strengths Affirmations and Abundance Activation

The subconscious mind is the complex underlying circuitry of our power grid. Our energy will flow and operate in accordance with whatever messages our subconscious mind tells it—whether positive or negative. For example, when we're stuck in scarcity thinking, we're throttling the power flow through our circuits. When we put all our energy into fear-based thinking, it's no wonder that we feel increasingly powerless to overcome problems.

Breakthrough, however, comes by learning to use your strengths to combat negative subconscious thinking patterns. In other words, telling your brain a different message produces a different result.

You can use your strengths to your advantage to steer your thoughts in the right direction. Sometimes it's a matter of "turning down" one strength temporarily and "turning up" another strength to produce the balance of energy you need. For example, take one of my strengths: strategizing about the future. When I was building my business and looking ahead (like I like to do), I sometimes began worrying if I'd have enough clients. That was my cue to turn down that strength temporarily because it was feeding my anxiety. Instead, I redirected my energy and drew heavily on another strength—my ability to be creative in my business pursuits.

I achieved this balance using an exercise I call Strengths Affirmations. Strengths Affirmations are short, positive, present-tense statements that you create that help you focus on how your unique strengths will help you achieve your goals. You can repeat Strengths Affirmations to yourself to rewire your subconscious negative thoughts. For example, my Strengths Affirmation I would tell myself when I felt anxious about future was: "I am creative, and I love to come up with something new." Another strength I have is producing excellence in my work. When I felt unsure about my abilities, I would remind myself of this strength and say: "I transform things from good to great."

What happened the first time I took these deliberate actions astounded me. Strengths Affirmations served as power switches, redirecting my energy from scarcity circuits to abundance pathways, from fear to faith, and from anxiety to excitement about my new business pursuits. My subconscious began to believe what I was telling it—and my energy followed suit.

Abundance Activation Practice redirects your energy toward your goals using Strengths Affirmations:

- Start by identifying your typical scarcity thoughts where you appear to lack resources, time, and/or opportunities.
- Recall your three to five strengths. Using these strengths, write your own Strengths Affirmations using short, positive, present-tense statements that focus on how your strengths will help you achieve your goals. These strengths-based responses should counteract each of the negative thoughts you identified above.
- Now practice redirecting your energy to one or more of these strengths whenever you're triggered by challenging circumstances. Repeat your Strengths Affirmation aloud or to yourself in those moments.
- Document the positive outcomes (versus focusing on the negative) to help rewire your subconscious. What results surprised you? Why?

- Continue to build your own library of Strengths Affirmations.

The key is recognizing that you are already equipped with the strength "circuits" you need. Your job is to keep them clear and powered up by reminding yourself of what you know to be true about yourself.

Tracking Your Energy Flow

Understanding your neural blueprint, recognizing energy zappers, and creating Strengths Affirmations are important first steps toward living out personal brand, Your Authentic Imprint. The real transformation happens through consistent, daily practice.

I challenge you to track your energy flow for one week by mapping your typical activities.

- Take stock of your energy level in the morning, versus the afternoon and evening. What do you notice about yourself?
- Now look at the whole week and begin to identify low-energy and high-energy patterns.
- What are you doing when you experience these highs and lows?
- Who and what contributes to these patterns?
- Connect these patterns to the three to five natural strengths you've already identified.
- Look for opportunities to redirect any low energy flow by drawing on these strengths.

Your efforts may feel forced at first but concentrate on the benefits that result when you make these adjustments. Spend some additional time with the Putting it into Practice section below, walking slowly and deliberately through each exercise. Just as a power grid needs regular maintenance, the following exercises are specific practices to rewire your brain and learn to manage your energy in the most productive way possible.

Looking Ahead

As you can imagine, a city like Singapore continually invests time planning for and maintaining its power distribution based on current needs and future goals. In the same way, you can implement specific strategies to direct your energy intentionally toward what matters most—to you! In Chapter 3, we'll explore your core values—the non-negotiable principles that guide your behavior regardless of circumstances. With a steady focus on your overall purpose for living, you'll see how core values complement your unique design and define how you'll live out your mission day to day.

~

Worth Remembering
Energy management isn't just positive thinking; it's intentional rewiring. By consciously choosing to operate through our natural talents and staying connected to our divine power source, we can make all kinds of changes for the better.

PUTTING IT INTO PRACTICE

QUESTIONS FOR REFLECTION

1. Which of your strengths feels most energized right now?
2. What activities consistently drain your power? Where do you notice scarcity thinking dimming your power?
3. What would operating from abundance look like in your current situation?
4. How might staying connected to your divine power source alter your daily experience?

EXERCISE 1
DAILY POWER SOURCE CONNECTION

Begin each day with time set aside to connect to your divine power source. Choose a consistent time and place to do so. Be quiet, still, and limit distractions. Start with 5-7 minutes and build up from there.

- Start with gratitude. Note three specific things you're thankful for. I encourage writing them down.
- Read over the Strengths Affirmations you've written.
- Connect to your divine power source through prayer, meditation, and/or journaling.

Keep a journal for recording insights you're learning along the way. Notice when you feel the most "connected" to your power source and record later how this sense of connection powers you through the day.

EXERCISE 2
DAILY POWER DIRECTION

Utilize The Strengths Journal (or any journal of your choosing) every day for the next 90 days. The daily habit of practicing an effective system will rewire your subconscious mind. Consistency is the key to achieving Daily Power Direction. Take 10 minutes or less to write in your journal:

- Express your daily intention and why you want to accomplish it. For example:
  "My intention today is to listen to others I encounter today, rather than react."
  "My intention today is to spend more time with the people closest to me at home."
  "My intention today is to keep my personal wellbeing in mind."
- Next, list three goals you want to achieve that relate to your intention and detail your desired outcomes.
- Finally, assign one or two of your strengths to help boost each task for today.

EXERCISE 3
WEEKLY POWER AUDIT

Here's another opportunity to put results in writing. Conduct a Weekly Power Audit where you think back and review your week:

When did scarcity thinking dim your power?
Which strengths helped you restore energy flow?
What abundance patterns are you building?

This isn't about perfection; it's about practice. Each time you redirect energy from scarcity to abundance circuits, you're building stronger neural pathways.

Scan to take the CliftonStrengths Assessment.
www.danawilliamsco.com/code

CHAPTER 3

Fueling Your Purpose: Identifying Your Core Values

I love how Colleen Barrett saw leadership. She was an example to many at Southwest Airlines, transitioning from her role as executive assistant serving the president to eventually assuming the presidency of the airline. She lived authentically each day, not seeing her title as important to her calling. Colleen mentored many people in business and in life, including me, and left behind a legacy of following The Golden Rule, treating others the way she wanted to be treated. Her heartfelt devotion to customer service was inspiring, and her wisdom will always resonate deeply. One phrase I heard her say more than once will stay with me forever: "Leadership is not a title. Leadership is a way of life."

Some of the most transformative leadership comes from people who would never describe themselves as leaders: the colleague who maintains unwavering integrity during a crisis, the friend who asks the perfect question that shifts your perspective, the community volunteer whose quiet consistency creates a space where others can flourish.

I've personally observed a young man with no leadership title in his day job take on the role of leading an entire volunteer group with remarkable vision and dedication. I've also witnessed a young, divorced mom create a safe haven by leading a community group, touching lives through her genuine care and resilience.

Then there was also the new employee at a nonprofit who transitioned from finance to mission work. In this new role, she embodied leadership from day one, although "leader" wasn't in her official title. She simply created that persona for herself and lived in authentic leadership. Twelve months later, she was officially recognized in the mission organization as a leader, but in truth, she had been leading all along. Your Authentic Imprint and how you "show up" in life drives everything about the legacy you'll leave behind. Recall our definition of leadership: **Everyday leadership is influencing positive change through your authentic presence and purposeful actions.**

When we embrace this broader definition, we recognize leadership opportunities exist in every interaction, every relationship, and every sphere of influence in our lives. They represent opportunities to serve others and to encourage, inspire, and help them. I've come to understand that true leadership on a daily basis isn't about managing others or holding authority. It rests on who you are as a leader—which then naturally determines what you do.

Defining Your Core Values

In short, core values define who you are. Values function as your personal constitution—the laws that govern your choices, even when no one is watching. They're not just preferences; they're convictions that define your character. They are your personal judgement of what is important in life. Values are a part of us, and they highlight what we stand for. They can represent our unique, individual essence and often come from a deeply held place—almost as if you "feel" in your soul the commitment and devotion to certain non-negotiables.

This is what they look like in the context of our formula for intentional daily living:

(Strengths + Core Values + Mission) × Emotional Recognition = Your Authentic Imprint

Core values are the principles that guide our decisions and actions. They provide direction when we're lost, anchor us in times of uncertainty, and help us navigate the most challenging situations. When we know and live by our core values, we act with integrity, build trust, and create a legacy defined by authenticity and purpose. In leadership and in life, our values are the reference points that keep us on course, no matter how turbulent the journey.

- Core values provide direction, clarity and consistency.
- Core values help you stay true to yourself when circumstances shift.
- Core values form the foundation for trust. Acting on our values builds credibility and connection with others.

- Core values are a source of fulfillment. Aligning our actions with our values fuels motivation and meaning.
- Core values form our legacy. The choices we make, guided by our values, define how each of us will be remembered.

Values in Organizations

Companies represent core values too. Although a company's core values are often overlooked at the grassroots level, that fact only underscores their importance in team development. Embedding core values into team-level work ensures they are not just abstract, high-level organizational concepts framed on the wall of the breakroom but are actively lived out by the team, contributing to a stronger team identity that customers can sense. Think about your favorite companies where you shop or eat. Which ones do you feel have clear, articulated core values? How can you sense those values coming through in your experience as a customer?

In my consulting work, I often see the power of knowing and applying the company's core values. They can transform a workplace—even in an already successful business. Sharing strong core values in a team is where the energy gets strong and people feel as if they are a genuine part of the greater mission.

Values as Individuals

As individuals, our core values also drive us forward in the same manner in daily life. Others can see what we believe and trace what's important to us by paying attention to how we behave. Values do several things for us:

- Help us make a greater impact by honoring our core beliefs
- Guide our personal code of conduct
- Streamline decision-making
- Help us connect with others on a significant level
- Help us maintain good habits and avoid escaping into bad habits

However, when you're unclear about your values, everything becomes more difficult. Relationships get overly complicated. Confusion reigns. Every personal and professional decision becomes more agonizing. You'll find yourself swayed by the loudest voice in the room or the most immediate pressure. But when your values are clear, decisions—even difficult ones—become much easier. You know where your boundaries are.

Being clear about your values and anchored in your strengths can also help you weather the volatile nature of our world. We are living through an incredible time of instability. Since 2020, the workplace and daily life have shifted drastically, thanks to the pandemic, economic fluctuations, and rapidly evolving technological changes like AI.

As the use of Artificial Intelligence grows, genuine human connection has become a rare commodity. Many of us find ourselves struggling to live authentically, feeling trapped in a cycle of conformity that leaves us yearning for true freedom. This disconnect can be particularly damaging, hindering our ability to excel in both our professional endeavors and personal relationships.

On the other hand, core values make us human. Pursuing a calling and living out what's most important to us breaks us free from the conformity cycle and puts us on a path that leads not only to professional success but also to personal fulfillment.

The secret lies in understanding and embracing your personal non-negotiables and your unique talents—and bringing all of that together. By building Your Authentic Imprint on the foundation of who you are designed to be and your inherent strengths and values, rather than trying to emulate someone else's beliefs about what's important in life and work, you unlock the power to be truly free. This authenticity is paramount to excelling in your work and calling, as well as successfully nurturing meaningful personal relationships. Here's the truth about the Internal Revolution: If you don't work on the inside, you can't change the outside.

But what if you jump into the Internal Revolution—and commit to work on the inside? Then everything about you externally can experience radical realignment from the inside out. Your goals. The energy you bring to your day. Your health, your relationships, your job. Everything.

Signs Your Core Values Need Attention

If you cannot articulate your clear core values—and stick to them consistently—you would benefit from clarification. The same goes for companies, since this truth applies in the workplace, too. Look for these warning signs of unclear core values—as you've noticed them in your life and/or at work:

- You feel constantly torn between competing priorities
- Your decisions tend to trigger regret afterward
- You struggle to explain why you made certain choices

- You find yourself frequently compromising on things that matter to you
- Other people seem confused by your inconsistent behavior
- You feel exhausted from decision-making, instead of empowered

The good news is that your core values and your natural strengths create a powerful synergy when aligned. You cannot leave out this important component in Your Authentic Imprint formula. It's not enough to just know your strengths. Strengths without values can lead to achievement without fulfillment. Values without strengths remain aspirational but ineffective.

What Are My Core Values?

Your top strengths hold clues to your core values—those non-negotiables that guide you through life. The reason why is because strengths by nature express certain corresponding core values. They go hand in hand.

The synergy between core values and strengths happens naturally in all kinds of settings. Strengths and core values overlap regarding who you are in the workplace—and who you are in your personal time. You're one whole person, you know—not two! What happens outside of work impacts our work. What happens at work impacts our personal life. The Internal Revolution is not about separating work from your personal life. Instead, it creates a holistic integration of your strengths and what you value at your core, on and off the clock, as one unified human being.

The following graphic organizes a word bank of core values into categories representing People, Power, Purpose, and Performance. As you study this chart, what words stand out to you? What core values are you drawn to in which columns?

Your Authentic Imprint Core Values

PEOPLE	POWER	PURPOSE	PERFORMANCE
Belonging	Achievement	Adventure	Accountability
Collaboration	Ambition	Balance	Accuracy
Compassion	Authenticity	Beauty	Commitment
Connection	Autonomy	Curiosity	Competence
Community	Boldness	Ethics	Consistency
Empathy	Bravery	Faith	Craftsmanship
Family	Communication	Fun	Creativity
Forgiveness	Courage	Growth	Dedication
Friendship	Determination	Hope	Dependability
Generosity	Excellence	Innovation	Diligence
Gratitude	Freedom	Justice	Discipline
Harmony	Honesty	Learning	Faithfulness
Humility	Independence	Legacy	Focus
Inclusion	Influence	Meaning	Improvement
Kindness	Integrity	Open-Mindedness	Preparation
Love	Mastery	Peace	Productivity
Loyalty	Optimism	Reflection	Quality
Nurturing	Patience	Security	Reliability
Patience	Presence	Self-Awareness	Resilience
Respect	Self-Determination	Significance	Responsibility
Service	Ownership	Sustainability	Results
Transparency	Self-Reliance	Truth	Stability
Trustworthiness	Self-Respect	Wisdom	Structure
Understanding	Success		Timeliness
Unity	Victory		

Let's look at the relationship between core values and strengths more closely. If your top strengths reside naturally in the

Relationship Building domain, you probably put a strong value on the core values listed in the People column including compassion, understanding, trustworthiness, and connection. These core values are what you crave in both the workplace and in your personal contacts and connections as well.

If your top strengths are in the **Influencing domain**, then you're likely drawn to the core values listed in the Power column. Things like integrity, authenticity, and communication are likely crucial to you. They often describe the other people you admire in leadership as well as your closest friends.

If your top strengths fall into the **Strategic Thinking domain**, you tend to prioritize the core values listed in the Purpose column including legacy, faith, and meaning. You place a premium on these qualities and can't imagine going through life without this context for the investment of your time and energy.

If your top strengths fall into the **Executing domain**, you're likely drawn to the core values listed in the Performance column including productivity, responsibility, results, and follow-through discipline. You're as likely to value these in your work environment as much as in your volunteer commitments. It may drive you crazy to sit through either a boring team meeting at the office or an HOA meeting where nothing gets accomplished!

The magic happens when you consciously begin to align your strengths with your chosen values. It's been said that your core values are the doors to your strengths. This partnership creates what I call "value-strength integration"—where what you stand for and what you're naturally good at work in harmony.

When you combine Strengths + Core Values, it gives you added dimension that you bring to your overall responsibilities in life and your overall calling and purpose. This is the Internal Revolution in action. It's how a genuine personal brand develops from the inside out and becomes better known as Your Authentic Imprint.

A Company Finds its Values

Alignment between strengths and values operates in whole organizations in similar ways to how it works for individuals. In a recent workshop with senior healthcare leaders, I introduced the Authentic Imprint formula to focus the team on their mission. (Mission is the third component in the formula, and we'll explore your mission much more in the next chapter.)

The most meaningful progress came when teams invested extra time ensuring their mission statements reflected their core values. Once members could connect the mission to their deeply held core values, the team lit up! The clarity and cohesion that followed were transformational. Core values proved to be a critical component in building the team's identity, aligning individual strengths with the collective mission and fostering a sense of purpose and unity.

But then something more happened. When they started matching their core values with their individual strengths, it all came together. They had a newfound team identity as they realized their individual Authentic Imprints. Everyone began to be aware of and respect each other's uniqueness because they better understood each other's strengths and core values (what was most important to them). For example, instead of thinking a co-worker who valued logical thinking was rude and off-putting for his direct manner, the team realized that he was just living out a strongly held core value for logic and strategic thinking. He thus became their go-to person for strategy.

Matching values and strengths produced a greater respect for what they shared in common—so much so that other departments began recognizing the uptick in the positive culture and team cohesion at work. Some people outside of that department even wanted to join their team! People were happier, they got along together, and they understood more about where the company was going.

How Core Values Benefit Us Personally

Once you marry your strengths with what's most important to you, you clearly start to see yourself aligning your personal brand with your authentic self and closing the gap between the two. How you present to the world gradually becomes more and more who you really are at heart.

You start learning how to craft Your Authentic Imprint that truly reflects who you are, not who you think you should be. These are just some of the benefits that result from having an Authentic Imprint:

1. **You Develop a Powerful Mindset:** You start overcoming limiting beliefs and values that don't serve you well. Instead, you cultivate a mindset based on chosen core values that propel you to success and fulfillment.

2. **You Increase Your Impact:** You can discover how to amplify your authentic voice and genuinely advance, support, and positively influence the people and causes that are important to you.

3. **You Network Effectively:** You begin to build genuine connections based on you being yourself—and appreciating others' strengths and values—in a way that supports your personal and professional growth.

4. **You Open Up More:** You learn to be willing to share your unique perspective and expertise. Why? Because you're more confident in what you can contribute to a common goal.

Creating a personal brand strategy this way is powerful. It's time to stop hiding behind a façade and start showcasing your authentic self. Remember, Your Authentic Imprint is your legacy that you leave behind. Build it with purpose and precision!

Do All Our Core Values Have to be in Play?

Monica is an extraordinary woman at the top of her game professionally. She moved from Mexico to take a job as a new HR executive for an international company in Dallas. However, despite having a job that utilized her powerful combination of strengths, she knew something was missing in her new life in Dallas. As our conversation deepened, I discovered that while Monica had built an impressive career and maintained close friendships at home in Mexico, she hadn't yet established her community in Dallas. She had a nagging sense of unhappiness as a result.

This dilemma revealed an important insight about her core values. Monica valued relationships and had a strong natural ability to win others over (in fact, it was one of her top strengths). So I inquired about her lack of community so far in her new city.

"Does it feel as if your energy is depleted because you haven't connected with enough new people here?" I asked, following a hunch about why she was dissatisfied. Her eyes widened with recognition.

"Yes, exactly that!" she said.

Meaningful connections normally fueled everything else she did. Despite her exceptional professional network and job satisfaction, Monica still needed to activate her desire for community in order to feel fully energized. It was that important to her unique makeup and could not be ignored.

We explored specific actions she could take, including taking classes that aligned with her interests, volunteering, and joining local community groups where she could form authentic relationships.

"Even though you're incredibly positive and successful at work," I explained, "by intentionally focusing on meeting new people through just one of these channels, you'll tap into a whole new source of energy each day."

This realization transformed her expression. She wasn't just hearing advice—she was acknowledging a key part of her authentic personal brand that she'd overlooked. Without giving attention to how much she valued personal community, she began to feel incomplete, no matter how successful and fulfilled she was otherwise.

Monica's story demonstrates how detrimental it can be to ignore something that's important to you—and maybe only you—but that's the point, isn't it? What's important to you and how you uniquely define significance and feel useful must be factored into your life's responsibilities and relationships. Without that, the engine that powers your life will not be firing on all cylinders. Understanding your internal wiring creates the conditions for your unique gifts to thrive and for your profound purpose to reach its full potential.

Leading by Example

Personal branding isn't about showcasing yourself; it's about putting your stamp on the value you deliver to others. When you walk into a room, when you take a job, when you make a new friend, when you join a community group, think about the impression you want to create. Is it based on the real you? Are you embodying your values through your priorities and actions? Are you inspiring and encouraging others by example?

Building your personal brand is key to unlocking the full potential of Your Authentic Imprint and creating lasting impact. It's the signature that defines how you're perceived and remembered by others. Personal branding is a journey of self-discovery unearthing the brilliance within and empowering yourself to shine brightly with purpose.

Exploring your core values is your opportunity to focus on self-improvement, leverage your values and strengths, drive your personal and professional growth, and have a life you're completely satisfied with.

1. **Visualize Your CEO Role:** Take time this week to imagine yourself as the CEO of your personal brand. How would you define your "company's" unique value proposition? Use language describing your core values to craft a clear description of who you are as a leader of others and difference maker in your circle of influence.

2. **Write Your Annual Report:** Set aside 30 minutes this week to write a one-page annual report for yourself. Highlight your values and strengths-based achievements from the past year and outline your vision for future growth. This will help you stay focused on self-improvement and set the stage for continued success.

3. **Make Strengths a Daily Discipline:** Commit to strengthening the tie between your unique strengths and your core values in some way every day. Approach that commitment just as you would a business practice, a new workout routine, or a healthy eating plan. Again, it's that power of daily consistency. What you do daily changes your life over time. Find ways to engage your strengths and core values in your everyday routine to refine and build your personal brand.

What Story Are You Telling Yourself about Who You Are?

Are there any goals you want to achieve that you haven't yet accomplished? It's inevitable that you have a list. Maybe advancing your career. Maybe starting a business. Maybe finding love or strengthening your friendships. Perhaps your list includes exercising and losing weight or getting into good habits. Our lives are filled with desires, and growth is a part of fulfilling them. So what's stopping you from reaching your goals?

Chances are that you carry a limiting belief (remember scarcity thinking, the great energy zapper?) that is holding you back, even if you're highly capable and successful. Most people have limiting beliefs, even if they're not aware of them. And it's a bigger problem than most people realize. Dr. Ethan Kross points to research suggesting that for one-third to one-half of our waking hours our minds habitually drift away to negative thinking about various topics, preventing us from being fully present and focused.[11]

In fact, you may may hear a contrary voice in your head whenever you're about to take your life's ambitions up a notch. That voice chidingly says something like, "You're not good enough to…" You know how to fill in that blank. In spite of your best efforts, this negative voice keeps returning, growing louder and louder. You need to deal with pessimistic input, if you want to become the kind of person you most want to be.

So how do you do that? Start by reflecting on any old story you've habitually told yourself about your limitations, failures, and foibles. Take a moment to consider the origin of the story. Return to your Life Map as a good resource. Where do these fears and limiting beliefs come from? The answers may be immediately apparent, or you may need to sit with this question a bit.

The good news is that the story you told yourself in the past likely does not reflect what is happening now today. You have freedom to create a new story loop instead—a story about the real you who is building a life on the core values you most want to emulate.

To start your new story, draw a vertical line on a page creating two columns. Write today's date at the top of the left column and the date of your 90th birthday at the top of righthand column. In the righthand column, describe the legacy you want to leave behind by the time you turn 90. What dreams will you ensure come true by then? What goals will you have reached? Who will be celebrating that day with you? What does that sense of accomplishment feel like and look like?

At 86 years old, my mother became the oldest graduate at Southern Methodist University in Dallas, proudly leading her graduating class as the flag bearer at commencement. Her children, grandchildren, and great-grandchildren watched in awe, inspired by her courage, determination, and unwavering belief that it's never too late to pursue your dreams.

What do you most want to accomplish with the time you have left on earth? In the left column of your piece of paper, you'll write your answer to the question, "What do you need to do between now and then to look back on a life of meaning?" Write down at least four big goals.

Review and compare your two columns. It's difficult for the human brain to believe something is true and actionable until it "sees" you start living it out. Whenever a limiting belief about who you most want to be creeps into your consciousness and threatens to delay or destroy your dreams, focus on your goals and tell yourself a new story instead.

Courage Enables Growth

You may agree with the principles you've learned so far. And you may even want to follow through on them. But do you ever find yourself procrastinating on putting your core values into action? A pinch of bravery may be what's needed right about now. Courage can skyrocket your efficiency in successfully implementing what this book is about: Living in your strengths, dominating your day, and transforming your life.

As I've pointed out, the Internal Revolution is not for the faint of heart. You may dread or feel unprepared for the difficult work required. Courage, though, is our secret weapon against our foes. It's not about being confident enough in yourself or totally fearless. It's about facing those fears—perhaps the fear of failure, even the fear of success, and, of course, the fear of change—and taking action anyway. Jenny Rometty, former CEO of IBM, once noted that growth and comfort do not coexist. Be willing to embrace discomfort as a catalyst for growth, knowing that true progress lies beyond the confines of your comfort zones.

Charles Dickens wrote in his classic book *David Copperfield*, "Procrastination is the thief of time. Collar him." That's right, we must tackle procrastination head-on by embracing our inner fortitude! When I first embarked on my own Internal Revolution, it took courage for me to step off the hamster wheel and believe that I could design my life and my days instead of letting them run me. Once I took that first step toward what was important to me, however, it opened up new ways of looking at how I was managing my day and my life.

At one point I even got to a place where I gave myself permission to admit, "I may never get to the bottom of my inbox! That's not 'me' and it's okay." When I embraced the truth about how I'm wired (instead of feeling guilty about not crossing everything off my list), I felt empowered to dominate my day.

You too are either living your days in default or design. When you live by design, you make a daily brave choice to embrace your core values. When you live by default, someone or something else plans your day for you.

When you begin to say "no" to the overwhelm and remind yourself to get very clear about what you want, then your outcomes begin to change. Here are three easy steps you can take today to put courage to work for you:

1. **Clarify your vision of a good day and then expect it to happen.** Take a moment to visualize what life looks like and feels like as you start planning your days based on desired outcomes. Your subconscious can't tell the difference. So plan each day with the outcome you want and why.

2. **Plan three goals you want to accomplish daily.** Draw on what you learned about assigning one of your unique strengths + core values to each goal to help you achieve your daily outcome. This exercise is part of your daily ritual outlined in The Strengths Journal.

3. **Create boundaries.** Healthy boundaries are crucial for your wellbeing, and they have a lot to do with your core values—we'll explore more about boundaries in Part 3 Transform Your Life. For now, just make a list of your non-negotiables you want to guard as you manage your day. For example, you might start with protecting your health from derailment by not working or scrolling on social media late at night, taking a proper lunch (instead of eating at your desk or in the car), and making time for some form of daily exercise.

Your Revolution – Put into action these three steps regarding courage. What did you learn about yourself in this exercise?

Perfection is a moving target. And we will never get there. Think of J.K. Rowling, another brilliant author, and the woman behind the worldwide successful book series Harry Potter. Before reaching superstardom in the world of books, she faced hardships and rejections, yet she didn't let fear halt her progress. Her courage was her greatest ally, and it can be yours too. Identify what you've been delaying working on regarding yourself and any associated fears fueling it. Commit to a courageous step toward completion of the tasks ahead. Reflect on how confronting any fear or hesitation you may have at this point can then supercharge your productivity in defining who you are, what you stand for, and what you most want out of life.

Looking Ahead

As we navigate a modern landscape where AI continues to reshape entire industries and career paths evolve at unprecedented speeds, many people find themselves questioning their professional purpose. Are they so easily replaceable? Will there even exist a place for them to contribute in the future? We all face an equal reckoning in deciding how to live with greater meaning day to day. So many are asking the same question on a personal level: "What am I supposed to be doing with my life anyway?" In this next chapter, you'll learn to avoid the typical ways people derail from their life's purpose. Instead, you'll craft a clear and actionable mission that emanates from your core values and one that you can act on every day.

∿

Worth Remembering:
Do not confuse simple with easy. The core values + strengths framework is what will help you learn and grow. It bolsters you when you face new opportunities, and it helps boost you to new outcomes.

PUTTING IT INTO PRACTICE

QUESTIONS FOR REFLECTION

1. How easy is it for you to make important decisions? Why is that?
2. Whose personal values do you admire? Why?
3. What benefits do you look forward to most when you implement the changes suggested in this chapter?
4. What daily practice are you doing now that helps you?

EXERCISE 1
IDENTIFY YOUR VALUES

Take a few minutes and identify your top 5 core values from the Core Values chart in this chapter.

EXERCISE 2
MATCHING CORE VALUES WITH STRENGTHS

Match the top core values you identified in Exercise 1 with your strengths and rank each pair in order of importance.

EXERCISE 3
REFLECT AND TAKE ACTION

Where are you overlooking a key core value that, once activated, could energize everything else you do? What specific action could you take this week to align your external activities with your internal wiring?

CHAPTER 4

Following Your Internal Compass: Knowing Your Mission

The rest of your life can begin at any stage of life. It's never too late to start the journey of discovering and living out your purpose and being your authentic self.

One of my favorite reminders of this truth is beautifully illustrated by one of the first and most successful American celebrity chefs, Julia Child. After World War II broke out, Julia began working as a young woman in the Office of Strategic Services (America's intelligence office before the CIA). She traveled the world, serving in Sri Lanka and China, before meeting and marrying Paul Child, also an OSS officer. When Paul transferred with the OSS to Paris in 1948, Julia made two discoveries. One, she loved French food and wine. Two, she really needed to learn how to cook French meals at home.

Julia signed up for classes at the famed culinary school Le

Cordon Bleu in Paris to learn French cooking techniques. Often the oldest student in her classes in her late thirties, she embraced the challenge and excelled. Where others may have just thought of French cooking as a hobby, Julia felt she had stumbled onto her true calling. In fact, she would recall having found what she'd been looking for all her life.[12]

Julia Child would then go on to become a household name. Her natural enthusiasm for preparing food and her willingness to try new recipes and embrace imperfection eventually led to opportunities to transform American home cooking. Instead of slowing down toward retirement, she released her first cookbook just before her fiftieth birthday and launched a remarkable career in television and publishing that continued well into her eighties.

Your Internal Compass

Connecting to your authentic purpose—your mission—creates both immediate satisfaction and long-term resilience during times of rapid change. Just as Julia Child's mid-life discovery created decades of meaningful contribution, we can prioritize living out our mission at any age. Multiple large-scale studies have found that people with a strong sense of purpose are substantially more likely to report thriving in their lives, with marked benefits for both mental and physical health.

The opposite is true as well. Without a sense of significance as to how we're filling our days, we tend to muddle through life. We're just existing, not truly living. That's one of the reasons why I sense the moment is ripe for more people to join the Internal Revolution movement. People are not satisfied to settle for less than authentic living. It's as true for those in the marketplace as it is for those whose calling falls outside of the office. I see it every day.

Some call this journey finding your "true north," and that's exactly the kind of language people often employ when attempting to describe an internal compass that keeps pointing them forward. Many times, they don't yet know where the compass is even leading. Devotion to a greater purpose is something they can't explain. It may be an interest that's never completely satisfied and one that remains endlessly interesting. It often shows up as a relentless curiosity about a certain field, world problem, or system. It also usually involves a nagging sense that they should be doing something other than what's currently occupying their time. It's that sneaking suspicion that there must be more to life. These are fluctuations of the needle of an inner compass guiding you to your life's mission, if you pay attention.

I've learned to be a firm believer in the idea that each person can dramatically increase their effectiveness and satisfaction in every area of their lives as they get closer to living out their unique mission. The key is our willingness to follow the guidance of that compass inside us and then make strategic course corrections along the way.

Derailed from Your Life's Purpose

Why don't more people live intentionally? I've identified five common ways people derail from the goal of living every day fulfilling their life's purpose. See which ones you identify with the most.

1. The Silent Mission Killer: Lack of Routine

Think about your most productive days. They likely had a clear structure that aligned with your natural way of working. Without a solid routine that leverages your strengths, you're constantly in reactive mode, responding to whatever comes your way rather than intentionally pursuing your mission.

By aligning your daily activities with your natural talents, you create a powerful framework that protects your mission from chaos. My most scattered days typically occur when I've skipped my daily internal work routine. I focus on internal work as part of my Internal Revolution early every morning to anchor that day's activities to my strengths.

In my coaching space, I want to own the idea that daily habits yield lifelong results. It's something I consistently emphasize with my clients. Those things that we practice on a daily basis are what rewire our brains and refocus our activities on what's important enough to deserve our time and attention.

If you want to practice a comprehensive daily system, stay tuned—we'll do a deep dive on it in Part 2 Dominate Your Day.

2. The Mental Energy Trap: Decision Exhaustion

Researchers estimate the average adult makes about 35,000 decisions each day. Each choice depletes your mental energy, leaving you drained when it's time to make mission-critical decisions. Steve Jobs wore the same outfit daily—he understood the power of preserving mental energy for significant matters. You can learn to quickly identify which decisions align with your natural talents and which ones might be better delegated or automated. When you work with your strengths rather than against them, you conserve mental energy for the decisions that truly matter and affect you and the ones under your care.

3. The Compass Problem: Unclear Boundaries
Success in life isn't just about knowing what you want—it's about being crystal clear on what you don't want. We must be clear on the areas where our limited energy might be better spent elsewhere. Did you know a compass needle can be damaged by magnets, metal objects, or electric current, causing it to malfunction and point in the wrong direction? Without clear boundaries based on self-awareness, you'll find yourself sifting through misreadings. Opportunities that look good on paper, but pull you away from your true purpose, point you in the wrong direction.

4. The Mission Diverter: People Pleasing
Here's a hard truth: every time you say "yes" to please others, you might be saying "no" to your mission. Understanding your strengths

helps you recognize when you're operating from authentic service, as opposed to fear-based people-pleasing. Other people might criticize if you go your own way, but your mission requires having the courage to disappoint others occasionally.

5. The Priority Paradox: Divided Loyalties
You can only have one true "number one" priority. Your strengths provide a natural filter for determining what deserves your focused attention. What you're learning in this book will help you align your daily priorities with your natural talents, making it easier to identify and commit to what matters most.

Which of these mission-killers is holding you back? One or more? Think about why this is happening.

What You Do Versus Why

It's not so much what you do that defines your purpose. It's knowing why you do what you do. Too many people live day to day without an inner compass driving the "why" behind what they do. It's possible for someone to be a totally fulfilled mechanic who is locked in on his mission of providing a meaningful service to others with his skills. On the other hand, you can be the CEO of an organization who climbed all the way to the top rung of the ladder only to find the job meaningless. The difference is found in the why. Why do you do what you do every day?

If you've ever taken time to craft a mission statement for your life, you know it can be a coin toss of effectiveness. For some, it is just a hastily crafted sentence—something that someone suggested. And then that sheet of paper made its way to the bottom of a discarded shoebox or desk drawer. For others, however, words on a page can spring to life and become the platform for intentional daily transformation that changes your life for the better. I vote for the latter.

Your mission statement is your why.   When done right, it is your chance to articulate your core values, capture exactly who you are, and determine how you personally define success. An ordinary person who wants to be an extraordinary difference maker can use a personal mission statement to their advantage in a number of ways:

- It can guide your decisions.
- It can determine your pace and make it easier to know when and where to turn, when to pause or even stop, and when to put your foot on the gas.
- It can ensure your personal and professional path remains aligned.
- It can help you develop and achieve personal goals that previously seemed impossible.

The kind of mission statement I'm talking about isn't just a corporate exercise—it's a personal declaration of purpose at the start of your Internal Revolution. Yet many people struggle with creating one that resonates with and guides their daily life. Why? In my experience, they often make these critical mistakes:

Common Mission Statement Pitfalls

1. Creating a Mission "Novel" Instead of a Succinct Mission Statement
Many people write mission statements that are too lengthy and complex to remember, much less live by. Your mission statement should be concise enough to recall in moments of decision. If you can't remember it, how can it guide you? The most powerful mission statements are often the simplest—clear enough to recite from memory and profound enough to shape your choices.

2. Crafting Someone Else's Mission
Creating a mission statement that reflects others' expectations rather than your authentic self is common—and dangerous. This happens when we focus on what we think should be important to us, rather than what truly resonates with our core being.

My husband's story illustrates this perfectly. When we met in college, he had spent his entire life being told he would follow in his father's footsteps as a doctor. His father had passed away two years prior, but the expectation remained—reinforced constantly by his grandmother who prophetically spoke of her grandson's medical future as if it were already written in the stars.

Despite excelling in pre-med classes and having a genuine interest in biology and science, something didn't feel right. After more than a year of dating, he finally confided in me, "I don't want to be a doctor. I don't know yet what I want to be, but I know it's not a doctor."

Somehow, I found the clarity to tell him what he needed to hear: he didn't have to be a doctor, but he did need to discover what truly ignited his passion. His shocked expression revealed how deeply ingrained this predetermined path had become. I had my own revelation hearing myself advise him to find and live out his passion. Where had that come from? I now know it was the flicking of the needle of my inner compass toward true north. It was an early sign of my passion to help people know their unique talents and use them each day—long before I made it my career.

In my husband's senior year, he finally gathered the courage to tell his grandmother what he'd told me: he wouldn't be attending medical school. He explained to her that he sensed something different waiting for him. That "something" turned out to be real estate, where he discovered his true calling in creating what he calls "cool deals." He found fulfillment in his Authentic Imprint on a path he never would have discovered had he continued following someone else's vision for his life.

How different might his journey have been if he'd had the tools to articulate his own mission and values earlier? Without the language and framework to express his authentic purpose, he nearly walked a path that wasn't his to travel.

3. Creating a Mission Statement Disconnected from Daily Life
A mission statement that doesn't translate into daily decisions remains just words on paper. Your mission should be practical enough to help you determine how to spend your Tuesday afternoon, not just inspire grand visions. In my workshops, we work on mission statements. If people's proposed mission statements do not sound unique or one-of-a-kind (like the individuals they are), I point this out. Why should their mission sound like anyone could use it? So what? Part of the hard work of mission statement crafting is that it must hold up when challenged.

4. Failing to Update Your Mission as You Evolve

Your mission statement isn't carved in stone. As you grow and your circumstances change, your mission may need refinement. The core might remain consistent, but how it manifests can evolve, as you'll see in Amy Purdy's story in this chapter. Those who refuse to revisit their mission statement risk following outdated directions, like a GPS missing a software update of the latest maps. Years ago when I began my coaching business, I thought of myself as a sort of purpose-driven midwife. Initially my mission statement read this way: "I want to help people birth their purpose and live in their strengths." About two years into my consulting company, I realized I needed to add "every day" because I was learning that honing your personal brand and creating Your Authentic Imprint is a daily work.

5. Crafting a Statement That Sounds Good—But Feels Empty

Some mission statements use impressive language but lack personal meaning. If your mission statement is so generic that it could belong to just about anyone, it most likely doesn't truly belong to you. A meaningful mission statement should feel uniquely yours—something only you could write because it captures your specific combination of talents, values, and experiences.

The kind of mission statement that manages to avoid these common pitfalls serves as:

- **An anchor during storms**—Reminding you what matters most when life gets hectic
- **A filter for opportunities**—Helping you quickly determine which paths align with your purpose

- **A source of resilience**—Providing meaning when facing setbacks and challenges
- **A foundation for authentic leadership**—Allowing you to lead from a place of genuine conviction
- **A catalyst for commitment**—Transforming discipline from a struggle into natural alignment

In today's rapidly changing world, a clear personal mission is no longer optional; it's essential for navigating uncertainty. Without an internal compass, we risk being swept away by external pressures and changing circumstances.

Mid-Course Mission Changes

Olga Romero came home one day from her corporate job and said to her husband, "I think I want to teach." She knew in that moment she was broaching a subject that would change both of their lives.

At the time, Olga enjoyed an exciting role in corporate communications at Southwest Airlines. But then an unexpected and pivotal moment occurred during a high-profile media event. The president and all the stakeholders and news organizations had gathered to hear the vision for an incredible future at the airline. Instead of feeling a rush of enthusiasm for a forecast of seemingly perfect conditions for the rest of career, Olga found herself questioning everything that day.

She recalls thinking, "This is all great! This is all fantastic! But what is my role here? Because right now I feel like I'm telling somebody else's story." Deep down she'd always wanted to be a college professor. She loved education and teaching.

But she'd have to return to school to get her certification in Texas. And then what? Why was she thinking about starting a whole new career while on the cusp of cementing her future at Southwest?

The dream of teaching wouldn't go away. She quit her job, went back to school, and set up her first classroom as a fifth-grade teacher at a high-needs elementary in the middle of Dallas. In her words, "Those kids changed my life."

Olga quickly rose through the administrative ranks in Texas education, driven by a deep belief in the power of education to create lasting change. Next, she earned her doctorate and led the turnaround of a failing campus into an A-rated personalized learning academy and helped launch Texas' first hybrid public school, blending in-person and remote learning.

Since then, Olga has served in executive roles in public education for entire school districts and also had the opportunity to teach at a university in the DFW Metroplex. Today her Authentic Imprint combines the best of both worlds—a strategic mindset shaped by her corporate background that's strengthened by her experience in and passion for the classroom. She is in her sweet spot now as a leader.

Olga faced many challenges along the way and learned firsthand the importance of mindset shifts, mentorship, and building strong relationships. And yet hers is a story of not only pivoting to a place where you're using your strengths but also how that shift creates positive change in your own life and in your community.

> **Your Revolution** – Can you identify a moment like Olga's when your natural talents pulled

you one step closer toward pursuing your true purpose? What strengths were you using at that time?

The Honorable Elaine L. Chao's journey is another example of how the pursuit of one's purpose can lead to mid-career corrections and adjustments. Consider how Elaine was able to scale purpose across multiple sectors and decades of service. She invested her life in a combination of public service, the private sector, and non-profit work—all with a single focus on creating economic opportunity for others.

She arrived in America at the age of eight without the ability to speak English. However, Elaine excelled in school and landed prominent jobs at Citicorp and Bank of America before being chosen to lead the Peace Corps and the United Way in the 1990s. Chao rose to even greater acclaim as the first Asian American woman appointed to a U.S. President's cabinet and one of only a handful of people to serve in multiple cabinet roles under different administrations. Her ability to amplify impact across diverse roles demonstrates how purpose can grow beyond individual achievement to create systemic change.

Your future dream for your life's mission can draw on everything you've experienced to this point. Everything's on the table.

When you scale your purpose thoughtfully, you create lasting change that extends far beyond your direct influence. Impact scaling simply involves identifying areas outside your usual sphere where your purpose could help and inspire others. It's even possible for your life's purpose to continue to impact others—even when you're no longer present. What we commonly call "leaving a legacy" after we die has its roots in living with purpose now. Your pursuit and enactment of your purpose and mission can change your life and create ripple effects that impact those around you. Long after your children leave home. Long after you retire from your job. Long after you sell the house and move from one community to start over in another. Long after you're gone.

Consider all the ways your life experiences, training, and the way you are specifically designed to think can enhance the lives of others—just by living out your purpose. Let me ask you something. How well would those closest to you be able to describe your life's purpose in a single sentence? What do you think they might say? If you leaned even more into your strengths, what opportunities could you create for the benefit of those around you, following Olga and Elaine's example?

A powerful mission statement isn't written—it's uncovered. Your true mission isn't something you invent; it's something you discover. It's already written in the unique way you're designed, the values that resonate most deeply with you, and the impact you're naturally equipped to make. Your job isn't to create it, but to uncover it and have the courage to live it out every day.

Four Steps to Creating Your Personal Mission Statement Framework

A mission statement is a concise, memorable summary of who you serve and the difference you want to make—it's your daily "North Star." But what if you don't know where to begin writing it? Or you don't want to waste time writing something you'll never use again? The following is a four-step framework for discovering and crafting the most practical and effective mission statement.

Step 1: Name Your People
- Who do you most care about serving? (e.g., leaders, teams, family)

Step 2: Define Your Positive Impact
- What changes for these people when you're at your best? (e.g., "they find their purpose," "they gain confidence," "they build strong teams")

Step 3: (Optional) Reference Your Strengths or Values
- If it energizes or motivates you, include how you uniquely create change (e.g., "through empathy and vision," "guided by my value of growth")

Step 4: Draft and Test Your Mission Statement
- Combine your audience and impact into one bold sentence:
  "I empower leaders to discover their strengths and fulfill their purpose."
- Ask yourself:
  Is it clear and memorable?
  Does it authentically reflect me?
  Would someone who knows me say, "That's you!"?
  Can I use it to guide daily choices?

Example mission statement: "I help [audience/people] [achieve X or experience Y] so they can [create an outcome/impact]."
- Optional: Add "by using my [strengths/talents]" or "guided by my value of [core value]"—but only if it helps make the statement feel more personal or motivating.

Sample Mission Statements:
- "I help teams work together authentically so they can achieve extraordinary results."
- "I empower young adults to build confidence and embrace their future."
- "I lead with compassion to help others unlock their true potential."

When I did this exercise, I filled in the blanks and came up with my personal mission statement: **I help leaders birth (my individualization strength) their purpose (my core value) and live as leaders (people I serve) in their strengths every day (impact).**

Your Mission Statement Litmus Test

Remember, your mission statement isn't just words on paper—it's the articulation of your unique purpose. When aligned with your strengths and core values, it becomes the foundation for a life of authentic impact and lasting fulfillment. Here's how you can ensure you're living your mission every day:

- Repeat it to yourself each morning to set daily intention.
- Reference it when making decisions or facing challenges ("Does this align with my mission?").
- Share it with a mentor or peer for external perspective.
- Use it as an anchor during stress or uncertainty.
- Revisit and refine it as you grow and evolve.

The Hula Hoop Principle: Defining Your Circle of Control

Like strengths and core values, finding and following your mission requires courage—the fortitude to look inward honestly and embrace what you find there. Sometimes you'll risk disappointing others who might have different plans for you as you step into the unknown to pursue your unique mission. Just as my husband discovered his true calling wasn't medicine but real estate, your authentic mission may likewise lead you away from the expected path. The temporary discomfort of this transition pales in comparison to the lifelong pain of living someone else's mission for your life.

One of the most profound lessons in my journey came from standing in my counselor's office, staring at a hula hoop on the floor. "Step inside," he said. Those two words began a revolution in my understanding. The hula hoop represented my circle of influence and control. Everything inside the hoop—my thoughts, actions, responses, and choices—belonged to me. Everything outside—other people's opinions, global events, the past—did not.

When you're not driven by your authentic mission and core values, you tend to try controlling everyone and everything around you. At that time, I had no idea that I had unique talents inside of me waiting to be unlocked and used. There was no playbook for this. But once you embrace the hula hoop principle, you instinctively recognize what falls within your life's mission and what does not. You realize whose dream you're living—and whose is falling by the wayside.

This simple visualization transformed my approach to life.

I stopped wasting energy trying to manage things outside my hoop and focused on what I could control—living authentically according to my mission and values. And I found a new freedom.

Is Your Purpose Future-Proof?

How will your purpose evolve as your life naturally (or unexpectedly) changes? You will certainly experience significant changes if you choose to join the Internal Revolution. We'll explore specific strategies for navigating change in Part 2 Dominate Your Day: but it's important to know what it means to have an adaptable purpose, since none of us can predict where life will take us in the future.

Amy Purdy is an award-winning American Paralympic snowboarder, motivational speaker, author, and advocate for adaptive sports. She is the co-founder of Adaptive Action Sports, an organization that promotes sports for people with disabilities, and she is the author of a bestselling memoir called On My Own Two Feet. At 19, Purdy contracted meningococcal meningitis, leading to septic shock. With a two-percent chance of survival, Purdy faced a wave of devastating consequences in the hospital: the amputation of both legs below the knee and the loss of her spleen and both kidneys, as well as her hearing in one ear.

Despite significant odds, she returned to snowboarding within months of her amputations, became a Paralympic pioneer, and transformed her challenge into a platform for inspiring millions of people globally through speaking and advocacy. Purdy demonstrates how someone's purpose can change course suddenly, and even strengthen, through seemingly insurmountable challenges.

Your mission can evolve as you grow. Revisit it:

- When your role changes significantly
- During major life transitions
- At least once a year during your personal review

This isn't about perfection; it's about clarity. Your mission should feel like putting on your favorite shirt: comfortable, authentic, and unmistakably you. The best mission statements don't impress others—they guide you.

When you future-proof your purpose, you anticipate change before it happens and create sustainable impact that grows stronger over time, come what may. One of the best ways to future-proof your purpose for living is to ground your mission in your core values—the non-negotiables that do not change, even if your circumstances do. After all, life involves change. And strategically navigating change is what we'll talk about next.

Working on Your Foundation

With your strengths and core values identified and your mission now clarified, you've built three of the four strategies contained in Your Authentic Imprint formula for intentional daily living. Let's review: **(Strengths + Core Values + Mission) × Emotional Recognition = Your Authentic Imprint.**

Think of these first three elements of the formula as your internal GPS system:

- Your **Strengths** are your natural routes—the paths where you travel fastest and with the most energy
- Your **Core Values** are your non-negotiables—the boundaries that keep you on course even when others try to redirect you
- Your **Mission** is your destination—the impact you're designed to make in this lifetime

But having a GPS isn't enough if you don't know how to read it in real-time, especially when conditions change. That's where the fourth remaining element of the formula comes in: emotional recognition. Emotional recognition becomes your magnetic multiplier and transforms static self-knowledge into dynamic, authentic leadership that adapts and responds to life's inevitable changes.

Looking Ahead

Throughout Part 1 Live in Your Strengths, we explored three of the four total elements of the Your Authentic Imprint formula. These three comprise a potent combination of your unique strengths, core values, and personal mission. Part 2 Dominate Your Day explores how you multiply those three elements together with emotional recognition that helps you reach maximum impact and effectiveness in your daily life. Emotional recognition amplifies everything you've discovered about yourself, turning your Internal Revolution into external transformation.

In the next chapter, we'll also explore the abundance mindset required to navigate the inevitable changes along the way as you live out your mission. The future presents challenges and opportunities for us all. Leaders and influencers must learn to embrace uncertainty and cultivate a desire to learn something new continually in every season of life. Change is our chance to foster learning and adaptation, practice deep critical thinking, and develop a nimble mind that can anticipate and not dread or fear change.

～

Worth Remembering:
Your Internal Revolution begins building momentum when you stop asking, "What should my mission be?" and start asking instead, "What is the mission I was designed for?" The answer to that question will transform not just what you do, but who you become.

PUTTING IT INTO PRACTICE

QUESTIONS FOR REFLECTION

1. How would you describe the "hula hoop principle" in your own words?
2. Why do you think most people don't live intentionally every day?
3. Name someone who is a good example of purpose-driven living. Why are they that way?
4. What excites you about the future right now?

EXERCISE 1
COMPLETE YOUR AUTHENTIC IMPRINT FORMULA

Fill in the following blanks using key words for your strengths, core values, and mission based on what you have learned in the book so far. We will learn more about emotional recognition in the next chapter.

(Strengths + Core Values + Mission) × Emotional Recognition = Your Authentic Imprint

(_____ + _____ + _____) × **Emotional Recognition** = **Your Authentic Imprint**

EXERCISE 2
REJECTING SELF-IMPOSED LIMITATIONS

Identify any self-imposed limitations that might be constraining your purpose. For example: "I don't have the resources to fulfill my purpose." Or "I'm too old/too young to fulfill my purpose." "I lack support from significant others to accomplish this." Why do you believe these are self-imposed limits? Are they real or imaginary?

PART 2

Dominate Your Day

CHAPTER 5

Emotional Recognition: The Multiplier That Changes Everything

"I'm completely drained."

This confession came from a senior leader I was coaching after he successfully implemented a major organizational restructuring. On paper, the change was a triumph—delivered on time, under budget, with minimal disruption. Yet the human cost was substantial. Not just for him, but for his entire leadership team.

Consider another real-life example. A mother of two teenagers is recently divorced and moving cross-country to start a new life. The changes looming ahead are daunting—new home, new schools for the kids, new routines, and learning the ins and outs of navigating a whole new city. The whole family is exhausted, vacillating between being excited about the possibilities and feeling overwhelmed and out of sorts. When will life return to normal?

Do these scenarios sound familiar? If you've been on the frontlines of significant change, you've experienced energy depletion firsthand, not to mention tremendous emotional upheaval in your attitude and approach to all the changes. One minute you're on top of the changes and handling it well. The next minute, you're doubting your ability to get through it.

Even leaders who understand their strengths and have strong change management skills still find themselves stuck when major transitions hit. Most leaders I work with today experience feeling invisible, overwhelmed, and stuck during times of change. They're spending 80% of their time on transactional items—endless emails, reactive meetings, mindless scrolling—and only 20% on the things that matter. They're living their days in default instead of by design, especially when change hits. They know what they should do, but something internal holds them back from doing it consistently. That "something" is often unrecognized emotions driving their decisions beneath the surface.

Your Authentic Imprint Formula Activated

For years I've been teaching people how to "Dominate Your Day" following the proven principles in this powerful formula: **(Strengths + Core Values + Mission) × Emotional Recognition = Your Authentic Imprint.** If you want to make a significant difference where you are, you must focus on that last part of the formula and include recognizing the emotional undercurrent of all your decisions and actions. Remember our definition: **Emotional recognition is the ability to notice, name, and understand your emotional state before it shapes your actions or relationships.**

Emotional recognition serves as the multiplier in the Authentic Imprint formula because it exponentially increases the power of the other elements (our strengths, core values, and mission). Without it, even your greatest strengths get diminished. With it, everything gets amplified. In essence, emotional recognition helps you become who you need to be to navigate life (especially during highly emotional times of change) with authenticity and strength.

The Hidden Cost of Emotional Unconsciousness in Leadership

Emotional recognition is not about being more emotional or letting feelings take over. It's about developing the awareness to catch what you're feeling in real-time so you can thoughtfully choose how to respond in a crisis or challenge, rather than just react. Think of emotional recognition as your internal dashboard—giving you crucial data about what's happening beneath the surface so you can navigate inevitable problems more skillfully. Most people, especially leaders, have been taught to push through emotions, especially during change. But I've learned one thing: emotions aren't distractions from good leadership—they're information for better leadership.

In fact, a recent Gallup study found that managers account for 70% of the variance in employee engagement.[13] Leaders who can notice, name, and respond to their emotional state before it shapes their actions create what I call "emotional safety" for their teams. Those who can't become unpredictable forces draining energy from everyone around them.

I learned how crucial creating this kind of emotional safety is when interviewing Eileen Collins on my Dominate Your Day podcast. Eileen made history as the first woman to pilot and command a U.S. space shuttle.[14] Rising from childhood poverty to become a colonel in the Air Force and a NASA astronaut, she commanded four space missions and logged over 5,000 hours in 30 different types of aircraft.

After the 2003 Space Shuttle Columbia disaster that killed all seven astronauts aboard, Eileen faced difficult challenges as the commander of the critical Return to Flight mission a year later. A surprising discovery in Columbia's accident report had revealed a problem that hit especially hard. Investigators cited a "broken safety culture" at NASA where people refused to speak up in meetings about potential concerns.[15]

Some might say that Eileen's greatest leadership challenge came not from breaking barriers in space, but from learning to create an emotionally safe place among clearly shaken space exploration teams back on Earth. As the new commander, Eileen spearheaded a culture where it was safe for every person to speak the truth to leaders, thereby multiplying the entire team's collective wisdom.

An emotionally unconsciousness leader might have discounted the power of Eileen's actions and just carried on into the next mission. When change and challenges disrupt your normal routines and energy patterns, it's easy to slip into default mode. Reacting day to day leaves little time for self-reflection, or intentional moments with your team at work or support system at home, or opportunities to invest in your own growth. You may find yourself busy managing the external demands of change, but you're not building internal resilience this way.

Living by design means recognizing this fundamental truth:

the solutions you need to succeed aren't outside you. They're within. Emotional recognition becomes your game-changer. Instead of letting emotions drive your decisions, attitudes, and actions unconsciously, you begin using emotional awareness to inform your choices. Learning to spot when negative thought patterns arise and saying "stop" is key to daily success in this area.

Life Map Breakthrough

Remember the Life Map exercise from chapter 1 where you charted significant events in your life and tried to spot patterns? If you haven't already done so, I encourage you to complete that exercise to help ground you in the practice of emotional recognition. When I first completed my own Life Map many years ago, I realized I was holding tightly to a scarcity mindset and had become compulsively busy—being productive but not being myself.

Looking closer at my Life Map, I discovered patterns of people-pleasing, control, and codependency rooted in childhood. I was "performing" but not truly leading. How exhausted it was to keep fighting old battles inside myself! It felt as if I were on the losing end of a tug-of-war rope, expending all of my energy tightly gripping pain, regret, and the need for approval—instead of letting go and choosing freedom from all that.

What helped me most, as surprising as it was to me, was the need to forgive. Unforgiveness was hurting me as a leader. When you forgive, you choose to drop your end of the rope. No matter how hard someone else might keep pulling, the moment you loosen your grip, the struggle finally stops. You're no longer trapped in that exhausting back-and-forth. Instead, you're ready to step into something new.

Through a process of honestly identifying harmful patterns, forgiving those who hurt me, forgiving myself, and accepting God's forgiveness, I was finally able to *release my end of the rope*. Forgiveness broke the old cycle and allowed me to step into new ways of living and leading—the Internal Revolution had begun. Only then was I able to build authentic habits. That's why I created tools like The Strengths Journal and now *The Internal Revolution*—to lead myself into lasting change. Freedom and authenticity are not the result of a single moment—they are made real through daily practice. Let these tools, the Strengths Journal and now this book, be your daily companions on the journey as you step into your own Internal Revolution.

Where on your Life Map are you still "gripping the rope" in an endless tug-of-war? Who or what do you need to forgive?

Again, I recommend finding an accountability buddy, professional counselor, or a coach as you work on your Life Map. Trusted partners can help you identify negative patterns so that you can name them, claim them, and then release them through forgiveness.

Burning It Down

Once I started recognizing how negative emotions formed barriers and limitations around my effectiveness in life, I knew I had to put a torch to them and start burning down those walls. From the moment I lit the first match, I felt lighter and freer. That's not to say my Internal Revolution and development of emotional recognition happened overnight. However, being in touch with my emotions (and being so ready not to carry them around anymore) transformed how I navigate every change that has followed since that time.

Every day presents a chance to test my progress, which is why I emphasize daily practice. Case in point. My sisters and I were recently helping our mom and stepdad move to a new senior living apartment. Everyone's old family patterns and roles came roaring back as I found myself and my sisters naturally falling into familiar behaviors that disrupted what we were trying to accomplish—helping our parents. Because of what I now know about emotional recognition, I quickly realized I was going to be miserable through the entire move if I kept up that old attitude and approach!

So I decided to take a timeout, process what I was feeling on the fly, and make a conscious choice not to "go back" to those old patterns. It's amazing what happens when we work on ourselves, instead of trying to change everyone else! We begin to experience true freedom.

A tool like The Strengths Journal helps leaders and influencers like you to build daily habits that keep you operating from your authentic strengths instead of old, limiting patterns, especially during transitions. What if you used a tool like journaling to set an intention for the day and began your day with five minutes of emotional recognition? For example, instead of starting your workday scrolling through negativity (e.g., social media posts or company news about organizational changes) and diving straight into crisis emails, tune in to your emotional state before your day begins.

Your Revolution – Let's say your company is restructuring. What if you checked in with your feelings before your first meeting about the restructuring? If you're facing change at work or at home, try asking yourself: "What emotion is present for me today? What might it be telling me about how to navigate this change?"

When you work harder on yourself than on managing external circumstances and go to your internal source for guidance, change becomes an opportunity for growth rather than just something to survive.

The Wellbeing Check-In During Change

Wellbeing isn't separate from your ability to navigate change—it's the foundation that makes sustainable leadership possible. During transitions, these five areas need extra attention:

Physical: Are you tired or tense from the stress of change? Recognize the signs before they become burnout.

Emotional: Are you anxious about uncertainty, numb from overwhelm, or frustrated with the pace? Naming it is the first step to managing it.

Social: Are you feeling isolated from your team or disconnected from your support systems? Emotional recognition helps you reach out and rebuild connections when you need them most.

Career*: Are you disengaged or questioning your role at work or in life as a whole? Use these emotions—however fleeting or confusing—as data to realign with your mission during transition. *Purpose

Financial: Are you stressed about resources or security? Recognize this as fear-based thinking so that you can respond with clarity, rather than a scarcity mindset.

Each of these areas ebbs and flows, especially during change. Awareness of what's shifting, and managing yourself accordingly, separates people who thrive during transitions from those who merely survive them.

Beyond Survival and Designing Growth through Change

Since 2020, society as a whole—especially the workplace—has shifted drastically due to the pandemic, economic fluctuations, and rapid technological changes like AI. Change fatigue is now a widespread and costly challenge. Recent research shows that 71% of employees feel overwhelmed by the amount of change at work, and nearly half of those experiencing change fatigue report increased stress and reduced productivity.[16] Leaders and employees alike are facing higher rates of burnout and disengagement as a result of constant organizational change.[17]

The people who emerge stronger from change aren't the ones with the most external resources—they're the ones who've learned to navigate their internal landscape on a habitual, daily basis. They've stopped looking for solutions outside themselves and started designing their growth from within, even when everything external feels uncertain.

A little disclaimer here. If things are feeling consistently "off" and there are outcomes you're not proud of during this season of change, it might be time to get some professional support. Sometimes the deep work of recognizing and releasing emotional patterns requires a therapist or counselor who can help you unlock what you've been carrying.

But the first step? That starts with you, right now, choosing design over default, even in the midst of change. It's about staying connected to your authentic self, recognizing what you're feeling, and using that awareness to multiply the impact of your strengths, values, and mission.

The revolution you're looking for starts within. Emotional recognition can become your leadership superpower, even in the most challenging of circumstances. Because here's the truth: When you combine an abundance mindset with emotional recognition, you don't just survive change. You design it. Remember the mantra: "Changing me changes everything."

Mindset 101: Your Internal State Creates Your External Reality

As we explored in an earlier chapter, most people operate from one of two approaches to life: a scarcity mindset or an abundance mindset. How do you know which mindset best describes you? An abundance mindset doesn't just happen; it must be intentionally developed step-by-step each day. And you're the only one who can do this on your behalf. You and you alone have the power to maximize your mindset. This is what the Internal Revolution is all about—transforming what's inside of you to help you put your best foot forward in life.

The science behind our understanding of mindset is fascinating. Researchers are learning the importance of something called neuroplasticity—the brain's ability to create new pathways and responses based on new information and experiences. Neuroplasticity is what keeps us young and our minds pliable and open, versus the tendency to become stuck in our ways and resistant to change as we age. That's why we must learn to manage our mindset through change and incorporate intentional practices that build new neural pathways as part of your daily internal work.

Your mindset during change is the lens through which you see the world around you. You can either optimize the power of a positive and clear mindset and achieve success—or you can cloud the lens with negativity that will destroy your dreams. I've learned firsthand that unlocking the power of your mindset can transform your life—one day at a time.

This brings us to one central truth that difference makers must understand: What you believe and expect doesn't just influence your experience—it literally creates your reality. Your perception of life becomes your life. When you're stuck, despite your talents and achievements, the barrier isn't external circumstances, is it? The culprit is the internal belief system running your subconscious programming.

What you tell yourself repeatedly in your mind during challenging transitions is what you become. In other words, tell yourself over and over how much you resent change at work or at home, and you become bitter. Dwell on the negative inconveniences of the change and you'll pine for the good ol' days too long and get left behind, stuck in the past. Emotional recognition helps you see your crucial part to play in how the changes unfold around you. It involves remembering to ask yourself "why" you feel a certain way, instead of just reacting.

Yet so many capable leaders feel invisible, overwhelmed, and ineffective. They're operating from outdated beliefs about their limitations, while at the same time desperately trying to create new outcomes. The revolutionary principle is that you can reprogram these limiting beliefs through something as simple as a daily practice of Strengths Affirmations, speaking energizing words that align with who you were created to be.

Neuroscience research confirms what spiritual wisdom has taught for millennia—the human brain doesn't distinguish between powerfully imagined experiences and reality. Every time you speak affirmations that align with your authentic strengths and values, you're literally rewiring neural pathways. You're programming your subconscious to recognize: "Oh, this is who I am now."

This daily work of belief reprogramming eliminates the old system that once dominated your decision-making. When you consistently speak what agrees with your divine design—your unique strengths, your core values, your authentic mission—you create internal alignment that transforms your external impact. The leader who masters this understanding doesn't just change their own reality. They become a catalyst for transformation in everyone around them, because authenticity is contagious.

How to Use a New Mindset to Your Advantage

What if three months from now you had an entirely new mindset and a brand-new lens through which you see the world? To get you started, I'll give you some strategies to strengthen your mindset and start making it work in your favor.

Strategy: Notice Automatic Thoughts and Responses
Start by paying attention to the automatic thoughts that surface when new opportunities arise. If you're asked to take on a new project at work, is your initial reaction excitement about developing a new skill, or are you overcome with defeating thoughts of possible failure? If a friend asks you to go to a new exercise class, are you already dreading it and feeling defeated before you even walk through the gym door? Or are you ready to jump in and give it your all?

Noting your automatic thoughts accompanying potential new ventures will reveal if you naturally prefer to remain stuck in your ways or if you're open to growth and change. A simple but powerful test in these moments is to pause and get curious about your internal dialogue. Ask yourself, "Is my thinking coming from scarcity or abundance?"

The other day I caught myself knee deep in the wrong mindset while asking my husband about a work meeting he'd attended. To my dismay, I later realized that every single question I had posed to him used a scarcity approach instead of an abundance approach. My scarcity thinking line of questions: *What went wrong? Who didn't show up? What problems emerged?* Contrast that to an abundance thinking approach: *What breakthroughs happened? Who contributed something brilliant? What possibilities opened up?*

See the difference? That small moment of awareness and course adjustment is an example of neuroplasticity in action. It creates a new pathway toward what I really want to portray in my life, including more authentic leadership and better communication with those who are most important to me.

Strategy: Journal Daily to Clean Up Your Brain
Each day, write down your thoughts, feelings, and the positive affirmations about your strengths that you learned in chapter 2.[18] It sounds simple, but by moving mental thoughts to paper you make room for an abundance perspective based on the possibilities instead of approaching your day with negativity.

I designed The Strengths Journal for the express purpose of capturing the compounding power of daily reflection and journaling. This journal guides you in writing your top priorities for the day, assigning one of your strengths to each, and then provides open space for you to write affirmations and other thoughts. Daily journaling organizes your brain to make room for a healthier mindset. We'll delve even deeper into this one life-changing habit later in the next chapter regarding productivity.

Strategy: Ignite Your Imagination
Your imagination provides creative solutions in the face of challenges. However, if I had to guess, I'd say the setting on your imagination may be stuck on "low" these days. For many people, the imaginative thought process is dimmer and quieter than ever because constant external stimuli (think social media, phone notifications, television binging, and the like) drowns out original thoughts and ideas that stem from your innate creativity.

If you want to reduce mental clutter, make room for more silence to welcome your imagination. Opt for a silent walk, rather than one filled with music or podcasts. Or set your timer for five minutes of free-flow journaling. Go outside on your balcony or patio, take a deep breath, and spend a few minutes clearing your head and paying attention to the details around you. What do you notice in the world around you? Igniting your imagination requires quieting the noise long enough for it to be heard.

Strategy: Adopt an Abundant Mindset through Service
A scarcity mindset rewires itself in a positive way through acts of service. Shifting from scarcity to abundance takes time, but the most fulfilling way to start this transition is through service. Serving others reminds us how much we have and how much we can accomplish on behalf of another. You have an overflow of talent and resources—and not for your own benefit. When we freely help others, we realize just how much we have to offer the world.

Amid the initial shock of being laid off from her corporate role, Sabrina found herself questioning everything she thought she knew about her professional worth. "I went from feeling valued, respected, and needed by my colleagues to wondering if I had anything meaningful to contribute in any part of my life," she told me during one of our coaching sessions.

But something unexpected happened while searching for jobs. As she began networking, Sabrina started asking people how she also could help them. She was surprised by how many people took her up on her offer. Board members wanted her expertise on strategic initiatives. Executives sought her guidance on projects they were launching. Instead of viewing these requests as distractions from her job hunt, Sabrina made a crucial mindset shift.

"I realized I was still solving problems and making an impact, even without a title and a team," she said. "Maybe I had more to offer than I thought."

One opportunity particularly energized her: helping a growing nonprofit organization develop a strategic plan. As she dove into the work, something changed. Her confidence began rebuilding, not because of what she was getting, but because of what she was giving. The scarcity mindset that had consumed her after the layoff began dissolving as she remembered how much value she brought to every situation.

When Sabrina finally landed a new job, she was delighted to discover that the company prioritized community involvement. Employees could choose anything, from back-to-school drives to ongoing volunteer commitments. Sabrina was drawn to a monthly program for adults with special needs—a dinner and dance event that has become the highlight of her calendar.

"The people are genuinely happy to see me every month," she shared with a smile. "I've learned their names, their stories, their dreams. What started as volunteering became real relationships."

Sabrina's story demonstrates what psychologists call "helper's high"—the neurological reward our brains provide when we serve others. Research at Emory University shows that helping others activates the same pleasure centers as receiving rewards, creating what scientists call a "happiness trifecta" of mood-boosting chemicals.

But the deeper lesson goes beyond brain chemistry. When we serve others, we stop focusing on what we lack and start recognizing our abundance. Sabrina didn't need a job title to make a difference. She was surprised to learn that she didn't need external validation to contribute value. Service reminded her that she had always possessed exactly what others needed—she just had to be willing to share it.

The experience also revealed something Sabrina hadn't recognized before her layoff. "I didn't realize how several areas of my wellbeing were completely 'off' because I was so laser-focused on work," she reflected. Looking back through the lens of Gallup's Five Essential Elements of Wellbeing, she could see the gaps clearly. Her Social Wellbeing had suffered, as all her relationships had become based on work. Additionally, her Community Wellbeing had all but disappeared once her children grew up and she stopped volunteering at their schools. She was also pouring everything into her Career Wellbeing (having a Purpose) through work but neglecting the social connections and community involvement that actually sustain that sense of purpose.

Work often takes place within a stifling culture of status and achievement. Volunteering cuts through all of that. "When you're surrounded by conversations about the 'right' car or job title, community involvement keeps you grounded in what actually matters," Sabrina explained. "Community involvement is so much more fulfilling and gives a long-lasting sense of accomplishment."

The most powerful insight came at the end of our conversation. "I will never give up on volunteering and networking again," Sabrina said with conviction. "Going through this transition taught me that community involvement isn't just nice to have—it feeds my talents and my wellbeing in ways nothing else can."

Sabrina's experience reveals a crucial truth about abundance thinking: Creating sustainable rhythms of service keep us connected to our purpose and our community, regardless of our professional circumstances. When we make service a non-negotiable part of our lives, we build resilience that transcends any single job, title, or external validation.

The measurable impact of serving others speaks for itself. Harvard research shows that those who give time or money are 42 percent more likely to be happy than those who don't give.[19] Even more remarkable is the idea that volunteering just two hours per week reduces mortality rates by 40 percent.[20] Helper's high isn't just a mood booster—it's a life extender.

When you're stuck in scarcity thinking about resources, time, or challenges, the fastest way out of the mud is through service. Not because service is noble, although it is, but because it's neurologically effective. Your brain rewards you for helping others with the exact chemicals that combat stress and create abundance thinking.

How Change Affects our Brains

Have you ever heard that change comes in waves? Surfers have noticed that "the big waves" come in sevens. They wait for six small waves to pass before the next big one comes along. The next big wave of change is always on its way in life. If everything is on an even keel for you right now in your personal and professional life, just wait. The next challenge is already on its way.

How you react to changes, great and small, reveals much about your mindset. This is the top issue I help clients tackle, both professionally and personally. Much of the time, we don't know what to do when a big change or wave of uncertainty comes along and crashes down upon us. But I can tell you what we usually do. At work, corporate change initiatives typically focus extensively on timelines, milestones, and deliverables. On the personal side when we're facing big changes (e.g., divorce, death of a loved one, sickness, job loss, moving), the advice we're often given is to "just give it time."

The unspoken assumption in both scenarios is that human energy is a constant, reliable resource. You just need to power through it and give it enough time, right? Wrong. Leaders and difference makers like to think we can do it all. The science tells us otherwise.

It's been shown that decision-making under uncertainty taxes more areas of our brain and requires us to draw on more cognitive effort when we're already feeling stressed.[21] You're not just imagining things—change really does make even the simplest of decisions difficult. Ambiguous situations also lead to mental fatigue. Studies in psychology and neuroscience have found they drain your willpower more than everyday tasks you normally perform.[22] Raise your hand if you've ever felt as if your brain hurt while trying to navigate a new task loaded with uncertainty about how to do it. Raising children. Dealing with a new boss. Even learning a new computer system.

Major change also does a number on our productivity. We think we can just keep going and doing "like we always have done." But it's been proven that productivity during transitions falls as we adapt to the new demands that come with life's changes.[23]

Over the course of my career, I've been through at least eight major re-organizations at work. Each one taught me invaluable lessons about protecting my own and my team's mindset when navigating change.

The first lesson I learned is how much it helps to have a clear plan to lead through change. Uncertainty without direction only breeds anxiety. Second, get buy-in early and often. We made this a priority by forming a group of "change ninjas"—enthusiastic individuals from every department and level of the group. This team wasn't just for show; they reviewed every proposed change and how to communicate it before anything was rolled out department wide, ensuring every voice was heard and considered.

But we didn't stop there. We also made the process fun—celebrating small wins, sharing regular updates, and making sure both leaders and change ninjas felt their contributions truly mattered. Right before we transitioned into the new org, we hosted a "speed dating" half-day event where everyone in the department rotated in 30-minute intervals with each team leader so they could ask questions and get a real sense of the new structure. This event wasn't just about sharing information—it incorporated connection and understanding.

We made the process of change fun, celebrated our progress, and created opportunities for everyone to give their input. These weren't just team-building tactics; they were deliberate strategies to recharge our collective energy and keep our mindsets positive and resilient. By the time we launched, people weren't just prepared; they were genuinely excited, engaged, and confident about where we were headed together.

What Doesn't Work

In addition to eight re-orgs at work, I've experienced countless personal changes as well. What I've learned through it all is that mindset and energy are inseparable. Each transition in our professional and personal worlds demands not only a new plan but also a new way of thinking to fuel this change with the energy we need to get through it. And therein lies the fatal flaw in how people typically approach change.

Typical change management in the workplace reveals an uncomfortable truth. During periods of significant change, traditional time management approaches like milestones and timelines (often issued from the top down) not only fail—they actively contribute to leadership burnout. "Chin up" and "just give it time" strategies don't really help us effectively manage the inevitability of changes in our personal lives either.

So what does work? Here is a hint—the solution has nothing to do with time, calendars, or deadlines. You see, the fundamental problem isn't time allocation—it's energy economics.

As we agreed earlier, it's more important in life to learn to manage your energy than your time. Managing and molding your mindset is much more than faking a smile or just positive thinking. It's about actively shaping the energy you bring to each challenge as part of your Internal Revolution. When you take care of your energy, you create the conditions for a mindset that can adapt, inspire, and lead through any change. When you approach change with openness, curiosity, and collaboration, your energy stays sustainable.

When I approach change this way, I find my energy levels are higher and more sustainable. I'm able to channel my emotional and physical energy into creative solutions, clear communication, and authentic connections with the significant players around me, whether personal or professional relationships.

Emotional Recognition and Energy Management: Your Leadership Revolution

On the other hand, stress hijacks your mindset, draining your energy faster than you can replenish. When I let stress or negativity overtake my mindset, my energy drains quickly. It's harder to show up as the leader others need me to be—at work or at home.

Not all human energy is the same. We don't generate it the same way, and we don't use the same strategies to maintain it. Managing your energy as you navigate life is not a one-size-fits-all approach. In my work, I have observed how human energy operates in four currencies:

> **Physical Energy** is your basic stamina and vitality. It gets depleted from burning the candle at both ends.

> **Emotional Energy** is your mood and emotional resilience. It drains from constant conflict or from suppressing emotions.

> **Mental Energy** is your focus, creativity, and decision-making capacity. It's often zapped by context-switching between responsibilities at work and home, especially during periods of uncertainty.

Relational Energy is your connection and trust with others. It depletes over time when relationships start to feel transactional, instead of meaningful and life-giving.

Emotional recognition bridges mindset and energy management of all four types of energy. Think of it as your internal dashboard, informing you about which type of energy is low and what intervention you need to power through your whole day. Most people, however, often attempt solving energy problems with the wrong interventions. For example, they try to fix an emotional energy problem with physical rest. Or they attempt to repair mental fatigue with more social connection. These well-intentioned efforts are like filling a car's gas tank when what it really needs is an oil change.

Let me illustrate energy misdiagnosis in action with the following examples:

> **Ashley, senior director during a merger:** Ashley found herself at the end of her rope, snapping at her assistant and drowning in emails. Her instinct to fix this physical energy problem was a physical intervention—trying to invest even longer hours at work. But emotional recognition revealed the real problem was relational energy depletion—she felt disconnected from her team. The solution was more authentic conversations with leadership peers, not more coffee!

> **Marcus, startup founder:** Productivity blocks led him to try task-switching (a mental fix to give

his brain a new focus). But putting emotional recognition to work revealed that task-switching was not the solution at all! He was lagging in productivity because he was anxious about an upcoming investor presentation. His mental energy was being drained by emotional avoidance. Once he processed the anxiety, his focus returned.

Lyle, executive: His energy-draining behavior wasn't ego—although it sure seemed that way. Negative. Self-centered. He came across to his team as "my way or the highway." The real problem, however, was unrecognized emotional depletion manifesting as defensive aggression. What Lyle needed was relational connection with his team, but instead of rebuilding connection with others (refueling his relational energy), he doubled down on controlling them.

Your Energy Audit: Questions That Reveal the Truth

Any time you sense energy depletion happening at a rapid pace, take a time-out to process a simple self-assessment.

First, do a quick mental review of all four currencies of energy. Ask yourself:

- **Physical Energy:** "Am I tired in my body, or tired in my soul?"

- **Emotional Energy:** "What emotion am I avoiding right now?"
- **Mental Energy:** "Am I mentally fatigued from complexity or emotionally exhausted from conflict?"
- **Relational Energy:** "Do I feel connected to people around me, or am I simply going through the motions?"

Next, process how you are currently "showing up" in the context of your helping and leading others. Whether on or off the clock, you can adapt these questions to your circumstances.

As a leader at work, perform a Team Assessment:
- What's the emotional temperature when I show up?
- Do people feel safe to be authentic with me, or are they performing out of duty?

As a parent, perform a Family Assessment with similar questions:
- What's the emotional temperature of our home when I get up in the morning, come home from work, etc.?
- Do my family members feel safe to be authentic with me, or are they performing to please me?

As a friend or spouse, perform a Relational Assessment with similar questions:
- "How do I affect the emotional temperature of this relationship?"
- "Does my friend/spouse feel safe to be authentic with me, or are they performing to please me?"

Matching Energy Type to Solution

Try the following solutions to patch up the energy drain you're experiencing right now.

> *Physical Depletion:* You might need rest or movement—but check first if you're emotionally exhausted and trying to solve that issue with your body. If you're getting plenty of rest and exercise, but still feeling emotionally exhausted, move to emotional depletion solutions.

> *Emotional Depletion:* You require recognition, validation, and expression of your emotions. You can't think your way out of emotional exhaustion—you have to feel through it. Possible practical solutions for emotional depletion include activities like: journaling without editing for 10-15 minutes to dump frustration onto paper; scheduling a conversation with a trusted mentor who can acknowledge the weight you're carrying; taking a personal retreat afternoon to process recent losses or changes, instead of pushing through them; or engaging in creative expression like singing or painting that allows for emotional release.

> *Mental Fatigue:* This kind of energy depletion often needs a complete focus shift, creative input, or strategic breaks. Surprisingly, sometimes the best mental energy fatigue cure is physical

movement or relational connection. Examples include getting some fresh air on a long walk or bike ride, calling a good friend to meet for a cup of coffee, or a combination of the two where you exercise with a friend or family member. You'll find that you can return to the tasks at hand with more mental clarity and focus.

Relational Depletion: This energy is often renewed through authentic connection, exchanging empathy, and having meaningful conversation. Beware—in order for this solution to take effect, it can't be faked or scheduled. Relationships require genuine presence. When was the last time you went on a guys trip or a girls retreat?

Here's a practical example of matching energy type to solutions. I remember working with Joe, a leader known for his strong analytical skills. During periods of rapid change, he often felt mentally exhausted from constantly re-evaluating every new piece of information. To better manage his mental energy and make the kind of impact he wanted to make on others, Joe followed our familiar formula for intentional daily living: **(Strengths + Core Values + Mission) × Emotional Recognition = Your Authentic Imprint.**

Joe developed a structured decision-making framework that worked for him. He knew his strengths centered on analysis. But before entering a change scenario, he would clarify his top priorities, set clear criteria for decisions based on mission and values, and identify which choices could be delegated or postponed. By using this framework, Joe conserved his mental resources—he didn't have to reinvent the wheel analyzing each new challenge. Instead, he approached decisions with greater clarity and less stress, freeing up more energy for creative problem-solving and leadership.

The leader who masters emotional recognition doesn't just manage their own energy—they become a renewable energy source for everyone around them. They stop trying to control outcomes and start managing their input. They are not energy vampires sucking the life out of everyone; they are energy multipliers.

Energy-draining leaders:
- React from unrecognized emotions
- Try to control others instead of managing themselves
- Operate from scarcity and defensiveness

Energy-multiplying leaders:
- Recognize their emotional state before it shapes interactions
- Take responsibility for the energy they bring to every room
- Operate from abundance and curiosity

Your energy is your message. What are you broadcasting? Your Internal Revolution isn't just about feeling better. It's about becoming the leader others choose to follow because your energy helps make them better versions of themselves.

Toward that end, before every significant interaction this week, I encourage you to pause and ask:

What type of energy am I operating from right now?

What energy am I about to bring into this room?

What does this situation need from me energy-wise?

By understanding emotional recognition and your unique energy economics, you will be able to transform your mindset and transition from exhausted change survivor to a sustainable change catalyst who has learned how to Dominate Your Day, every day.

The Complete Formula

There you have it—all four elements of Your Authentic Imprint formula that work in harmony to help you find and live out the "real you." How can you best use Your Authentic Imprint?

- In leadership positions, use it to uncover where you are flourishing versus where you may feel misaligned or depleted.
- When faced with tough decisions, ask: "Which part of my Authentic Imprint do I need to lean into right now?"
- Use the emotional recognition piece to shift from default, reactive leadership to intentional, presence-driven leadership.
- Revisit quarterly or annually as part of personal and/or leadership development planning.

The Authentic Imprint framework is a holistic model for self-discovery, leadership presence, and transformation. It integrates your best strengths, deepest values, core purpose, and emotional self-awareness—defining how you uniquely lead and inspire. It works—when you reinforce its principles daily.

I'm reminded once more of a daily discipline practiced by astronaut and pilot Eileen Collins. Great leaders—like great pilots—don't leave emotional steadiness, clarity, or purpose to chance. Before every flight, even after her years of experience, Eileen anchored herself with a checklist. The ritual wasn't just about procedures; it was her system for tuning into the mission, managing nerves, and centering her mind—especially under stress.

Just as pilots use checklists to manage complexity and pressures, reviewing your strengths, values, mission, and emotional state every day is essential. The most extraordinary growth comes not from a flash of inspiration, but from small, intentional rituals repeated every day.

Daily Authentic Imprint Checklist

Step 1: Unlock Your Strengths
- List 5-10 unique talents or strengths from Chapter 2 (using CliftonStrengths or personal reflection).
- What energizes you? Where do you consistently excel?

Step 2: Identify Your Core Values
- Choose your 5 most important guiding values (for a refresher, consult the Your Authentic Imprint Core Values chart in Chapter 3).
- What principles do you stand for, no matter what?

Step 3: Clarify Your Mission

- Use the 4-Step Mission Statement process from Chapter 4 to articulate your core purpose.

Step 4: Multiply with Emotional Recognition

- Build daily habits of emotional self-awareness from Chapter 5:
  - Each morning: "What energy am I bringing today?"
  - During the day: "What do my people need emotionally in this moment?"
  - Evenings: "What feeling did I leave behind today?"
- Learn your own energy "currencies" (physical, emotional, mental, relational) and match your self-care appropriately.

Step 5: Apply the Formula:

(Strengths + Core Values + Mission) × Emotional Recognition
= Your Authentic Imprint

- Recognize that Your Authentic Imprint is maximized when you:
  - Lead from your strengths
  - Live according to your values
  - Stay grounded in purpose
  - And multiply all this through active emotional recognition

Authenticity happens at the intersection of self-awareness (knowing your strengths, values, and mission) and awareness of others (using emotional recognition to connect and lead). Put it all together and you have a plan you're living out every day. Even if it's three steps forward and two steps back, keep going forward. When you lead from Your Authentic Imprint, you don't just adapt to change—you take the initiative to create the perfect improvements, enhancements, and upgrades during change. You don't just manage people—you inspire them. You not only achieve results but also leave a legacy.

Looking Ahead

Chapter 6 is not about productivity in the traditional sense of "how to get more done in less time." In fact, this chapter presents the exact opposite, and hopefully it reframes how you think about productivity as a whole. My quest to understand what it meant to be truly effective in life did not evolve during a period of particularly intense activity and responsibility in my life. Believe it or not, the idea came to me when I was asleep.

Worth Remembering
We must understand how emotional recognition amplifies our strengths, core values, and mission and makes us more effective—especially during life's changes. The problem isn't necessarily the change itself, it's when we approach change with traditional time management strategies, instead of energy management. When you have the right mindset and work through your natural pattern of talents (the things that energize rather than drain you), you create energy to power through your day instead of just consuming it.

PUTTING IT INTO PRACTICE

QUESTIONS FOR REFLECTION

Daily Check-In:

- What emotion is most present for me today as I navigate this change?
- What might this emotion be telling me about what needs my attention?
- Which one of my four energy currencies (physical, emotional, mental, relational) feels the most depleted right now?
- How can I use my unique strengths to address what I'm feeling instead of just pushing through?
- What's one way I can design my response to today's challenges rather than just reacting?

Weekly Reflection:

- Where am I still looking for external solutions to internal challenges during this transition?
- How has my emotional recognition evolved since last week?
- What growth am I designing through this change, rather than just trying to survive it?

EXERCISE 1
CONDUCT DAILY ENERGY AUDITS

What activities connected to your natural talents consistently energize you, even during disruption? These aren't just activities you enjoy, they're activities that align with how you naturally think, feel, and behave. When you identify these, you've found your energy source.

EXERCISE 2
ESTABLISH "STABILITY ZONES"

A stability zone is any practice, environment, or relationship you deliberately protect from change. This might be a morning ritual you never skip, a weekly team check-in with a consistent format, or even a physical workspace arrangement you maintain despite everything else shifting. These zones become your reliable anchors during turbulence.

EXERCISE 3
PRACTICE STRENGTHS RECOVERY

Deliberately engage your natural talents in small ways when you're feeling depleted. Even 15 minutes can make a difference.

CHAPTER 6

Productivity: Leveraging Your Strengths Daily

I once had a vivid dream about not being able to get into my house. In my dream, our front door was locked, and I was standing at the keypad desperately trying every four-digit combination I could think of. But nothing worked. I pounded on the door, but no one heard me. Being locked out of my own home and unable to enter was frustrating. I finally leaned against the doorframe and slowly slid down, exhausted and wondering how I would ever figure out the elusive code to open the door. Then, clear as day, I heard the answer: "You already have the code. It's L-O-V-E."

I woke up with tears in my eyes and a truth that would reshape what I thought I knew about authentic leadership. My dream wasn't just about a door security code. It was pointing me toward how to access my authentic self on a daily basis and how to live in love every day.

At that point, I had been teaching others for years about strengths, values, mission, and emotional recognition—all the external frameworks of being a more productive and authentic person. But the dream warned me not to overlook the foundation that makes it all work: love. Not the soft, sentimental kind, but the revolutionary act of loving yourself the way you were created to be loved and loving others in the same manner.

The question I then posed was significant: "What if everything I've been taught (and have been teaching!) about productivity is backwards?" For decades, leadership culture and self-help gurus have worshipped at the altar of "doing more." More effort, more meetings, more projects, more hours, more speed. Somewhere along the way, we confused motion with progress, activity with achievement, and busyness with significance.

But then groundbreaking researchers and thousands of authentically transformed people put this older theory to the test. They revealed a startling truth. When you do internal work on yourself, everything external begins to shift into high gear. The most productive leaders aren't doing more—they're being more authentic in pursuit of what matters and accomplishing more than ever.

Love Transforms the Formula

Without love as the foundation, the formula for intentional daily living runs the risk of producing lifeless performance-based productivity, not living and breathing authenticity.

However, when you love your authentic self—really love who you were created to be and extend to others the same courtesy—there's a seismic shift in how you order your day and therefore your life.

You begin designing your day and gain a more well-rounded schedule that prioritizes what is most important according to your particular wiring. That's the Internal Revolution in action. I now know I have to reserve daily time for myself and time with my friends and family. If I'm not being replenished this way, I'm not accomplishing much no matter how many hours there are in a day.

I wish I'd read about this in a book years ago when I was first trying to find my authentic self. I see how this principle connects with my contemporaries today in a number of industries who are leaving their current role in the corporate world in search of their authentic self. They were wildly successful after decades at iconic businesses like American Express and AT&T, but at the same time they were deeply unhappy.

A fellow coach I met last year was a corporate leader of a national organization. Her GenX work ethic called for pounding it out at the office five days a week, much like our parents did. I often see this carryover among Gen X and some Millennials with this same inherited work ethic. When she realized a traditional approach to a career would not allow her to embrace her family needs, she resigned and eventually created her own media company from scratch. Today she helps others in the tech industry using her true strengths, core values, and mission.

If you want to go find yourself, I jokingly say quitting your job and starting your own company is a good way to do that in a hurry! You come face to face with who you really are at that particular crossroads.

There is a revolutionary truth involved in every Internal Revolution and it's this: The heart is infinitely greater than the mind whenever we're pursuing authentic transformation. We cannot strategize our way into authenticity. We cannot think our way into loving ourselves and others. The heart must lead. South African writer, teacher, and pastor Andrew Murray said it this way: "My mind is utterly impotent in creating and maintaining a spiritual life within me; the heart must wait on God to do that work within me."[24]

You'll know you're incorporating love (for self and others) into your formula for intentional daily living when you see the following evidence begin to appear in each component.

(Strengths + Core Values + Mission) × Emotional Recognition = Your Authentic Imprint

> **Strengths** become gifts you offer freely, not tools you wield for approval. You stop hiding your unique talents because they don't fit someone else's definition of leadership, and you start celebrating how you're uniquely wired to make a difference. Trusting your heart requires you to love and appreciate what you find there, even the parts that don't fit conventional leadership models.

> **Core values** become non-negotiables you honor, not ideals you perform. You stop compromising what matters most to you (in an effort to keep others comfortable). Instead, you start living with the integrity that attracts the right people

and opportunities, leading to true satisfaction at the end of each day.

Mission becomes the calling you pursue, not the image you project. You stop chasing what looks impressive and start building what matters, driven by a passion for making the kind of impact on your circle of influence that only you can make.

Emotional recognition, the great multiplier of all of the above, then ensures that you are responding from love, not reacting from fear of other people's responses. You learn to recognize whenever you're inadvertently operating from busyness and old people-pleasing patterns or if you're responding from the deep love and security of knowing who you are.

Love doesn't just improve the formula for intentional daily living—it takes over and revolutionizes it. Love transforms you from trying to be someone you think you should be to someone who maximizes their effectiveness every day by living and leading from the inside out.

Ancient wisdom from a proverb summarizes it perfectly: Trust with your whole heart, not your own mind.[25] For leaders, this means trusting that who you authentically are—your unique wiring, your specific calling, your individual way of making a difference—is not only enough (and productive) but also exactly what the world needs.

The Oxygen Mask Principle

In my 25 years in the airline industry, I heard the safety announcement thousands of times: "Put your own oxygen mask on first before helping others." That principle is often used outside of aviation to mean that we must take care of ourselves before we can help others. Most leaders nod their approval of this familiar axiom and then completely ignore it.

You cannot give what you don't have. You cannot love others authentically if you haven't learned to love yourself. You cannot attract the right team, the right opportunities, or the right kind of success if you're operating from an empty tank, desperately trying to prove your worth through external achievement. Show me your completed to-do list, but without love motivating your actions, it's ultimately meaningless. I remember well my early days of naively thinking I was "getting so much done" while putting myself last. From the perspective of the casual observer, I was serving others beautifully by putting their oxygen masks on first. Yet I was suffocating myself in the process.

The most revolutionary thing you can do as an influencer of others is to learn to love yourself—not in a narcissistic way, but in the way that recognizes you are fearfully and wonderfully made, with unique gifts that the world needs. This isn't selfish self-love; it's essential to survival. When you operate from this foundation of love, you become a magnet for others who are also committed to authentic excellence.

The Daily Work of Love

It takes consistent practice to learn to love yourself as you are, unconditionally, with grace, patience, and acceptance. This isn't a one-time decision; it's a daily choice to show up for yourself the way you desire to show up for others. In fact, that choice is the key to Dominating Your Day, and it's why I encourage daily practice to accomplish this transformational work. Every 24 hours, you're invited to turn the traditional understanding of productivity on its ear and tune into a new daily practice based on loving how you're designed.

Yes, you have so much to do every day. But take time to start and end your day with the daily work of loving yourself. Suggestions include:

- Emotional Recognition Check-in (start of day): How are you feeling?
- Authentic Imprint Reflection (end of day): Where did your strengths, values, and mission align today? What are you grateful for? What did you learn? What do you want to do differently tomorrow?

The goal isn't perfection—it's presence. It's you being present to who you are, present to how you're growing, and present to the love that makes transformation possible. The difference is creating significance, not crossing off items on to-do lists. This is not productivity as we used to know it. Surprise—it's not about "doing more" when you Dominate Your Day! Your steady focus is instead on defeating old patterns and reactive habits with the intentional daily work of love.

I've often admired how monks start every new day by reviewing the day before. The question is, "How did I live yesterday?" versus "What did I get done yesterday?" Reflecting on the good finish of a day is the best predictor of having a good start to the next day. I love how my editor's Norwegian husband often asks in the evening, "Are you satisfied with the day?" Not, how much did you "get done"? But are you satisfied? That's a whole other question, isn't it?

Micro-Moments That Transform Leadership

Real transformation doesn't happen in annual retreats or quarterly planning sessions. It happens in the micro-moments throughout your day when you catch yourself falling into old patterns—then you consciously choose your authentic response instead. These moments are foundational to your Internal Revolution—the split-second decisions where you stop feeding who you used to be and start nourishing who you were created to become. If you want to be more productive in the ways that count, this step is essential mastery.

Every person faces dozens of these micro-moments daily. The email that makes your jaw clench. The meeting where you feel yourself shrinking. The conversation where old insecurities whisper familiar lies. The decision where you feel pressure to choose what looks or sounds good over what feels right. As we explored in Chapter 5, your brain does not know the difference between a powerfully imagined experience and reality. Therefore, every time you choose your authentic response over your old reactive pattern, you're literally rewiring your neural pathways. You're programming your subconscious to recognize each choice not as a stressful moment to avoid but a revolutionary opportunity to embrace.

Jennifer, a vice president of marketing, experienced one such opportunity. As part of her Internal Revolution, she realized that she'd built a career habitually and subconsciously apologizing for her expertise, diminishing her ideas before anyone else could do so. In fact, she automatically started every presentation with "Sorry to take up your time, but..."

Then she began identifying her strengths and applying them. Still, during the next crucial budget meeting, Jennifer once more felt that familiar urge to minimize her proposal. But instead of launching into her usual apologetic preamble, she paused. Took a breath. And asked herself: "What would confidence look like right now?" She remembered her top strength was the ability to see connections others missed. That wasn't something to apologize for—it was exactly what the room needed.

"Here's what I'm seeing that could change everything for us," she began instead.

The energy in the room shifted immediately. Jennifer's idea was approved unanimously. That 30-second choice to feed her authentic confidence through her unique strength, instead of her old apologetic pattern, became Jennifer's Internal Revolution moment. A year later, she was promoted to senior vice president.

Leveraging your strengths daily is a productivity enhancer. Instead of making a to-do list, ask yourself: "What's getting in my way and what strength can I use to navigate myself out of it?"

Daily Emotional Recognition Practice for Leaders

Here's where you draw on your emotional recognition skills as part of a new way to think about productivity and accomplishment. Recall our definition: **Emotional recognition is the ability to notice, name, and understand your emotional state before it shapes your actions or relationships.**

This requires consistent daily practice, like a pilot checking off a checklist. It's not just crisis management. It's presence, not perfection; responsive leadership, instead of reactive management. Use this three-level approach to develop your responsive leadership muscle and position yourself to achieve more significant work every day:

> **Morning Check-In (Level 1)** "What energy am I bringing to strategic work today?"
> Start your day with intentional energy awareness.

> **Real-Time Awareness (Level 2)** "What does this situation need from me?"
> Respond to challenges from presence, not patterns.

> **Evening Reflection (Level 3)** "What did I leave people with regarding our strategic direction?"
> Assess your leadership impact, not just your productivity.

Here's the crucial part: don't just choose the new response—actively burn the old pattern. When you catch yourself about to react from insecurity, literally visualize that old pattern going up in flames. Give your mind a clear visual signal: "I don't live there anymore."

Replace rumination with revolution.

The Revolution Ripple Effect

The most powerful part of the Internal Revolution isn't just personal transformation—it's the ripple effect. When you stop reacting from old patterns and start responding from your authentic strengths, everyone around you notices.

Your team stops walking on eggshells because you've stopped bringing your triggers to work. Your colleagues start bringing their real ideas because you've modeled authentic confidence. Your family and friends get the real you instead of the stressed, reactive version.

You'll know you're successfully living your Internal Revolution when old triggers lose their power. You are not addicted to chaos anymore. That criticism that used to send you spiraling now feels like information. That rejection that used to devastate you now feels like redirection. That pressure that used to overwhelm you now feels like energy. The goal isn't how to avoid being stressed. Stress is inevitable in life. The challenge is to respond to stress using Your Authentic Imprint, instead of your old programming.

> **Your Revolution** – Set aside some time to complete these steps this week.

> **Step 1 – Identify Your Pattern:** What's one reactive pattern you notice in yourself? (needless

apologizing, people-pleasing, getting defensive, shutting down, etc.)

Step 2 – Practice Today: Set an intention to catch yourself in that old pattern once today and try your chosen revolution technique instead.

Step 3 – Track Your Wins: In your evening journal reflection, note any Internal Revolution moments you experienced as a result.

Instead of analyzing why you feel triggered in the moment, exercises like these help you invest that mental energy in strengthening your authentic response. **You don't need to be more productive—you need to be more you.** And "more you" happens one authentic choice at a time, all day long. The Internal Revolution isn't coming. The Internal Revolution is now. It's in this moment, and the next one, and the one after that. You get to choose who you become, one micro-moment at a time.

You Attract Who You Are, Not What You Want

I recently watched a founder completely torpedo a strategy call by a lack of love. When someone said black, "Mark" said white. His negativity was toxic, and it was astonishing to witness how this single person's pessimism could fill the room. So laser-focused on his message, he became tone-deaf to everyone else's input. With his "my way or the highway" operating system, everyone was drained at the end of the call because naysaying energy had sucked the life out of the room.

But what was Mark trying to accomplish? Like most leaders, I'm sure he wanted to attract engaged team members and ironically thought this was a good way to go about doing so. However, what he wanted—and what happened—were two different stories.

I've learned a valuable principle after years of coaching successful leaders. You attract who you are, not what you want. No matter how hard you try, lack of emotional recognition attracts the very opposite of what you want—people mentally checking out. Whether we are leaders of a team or a family, whenever we're operating without emotional recognition we lose people. If you want engaged, innovative, committed people around you in any setting, become the kind of leader whose energy multiplies rather than diminishes others. This insight stops most leaders in their tracks because they intuitively know it's true, and they're terrified by what it means. It means taking a good look at the significant others in your work and home life, your opportunities, and even your challenges. They're all mirrors reflecting who you currently are, not who you're trying to become or what you're desperately wanting to achieve.

If your desire is for a healthy family, lead as the kind of parent who brings out the best in others. Don't zap the good vibes in your family with unrealistic demands and constant correction.

If your desire is for a better working relationship with others at work, be the kind of teammate who looks for win-win solutions.

If your desire is for the people on your community volunteer board, your church, or your small group to function well and accomplish what they're called to do, live and lead in such a way that honors that ideal.

The people-pleaser attracts more people to please. The perfectionist attracts more impossible standards. The leader operating from scarcity attracts more scarcity. I lived this reality for years. As someone who spent decades perfecting the art of being the "good girl"—doing what others expected, I reacted the way I thought people wanted me to react. And I was attracting exactly that: more expectations, more pressure to perform, more situations that demanded I be someone other than who I truly was. I was always busy, but not necessarily always productive.

Most leaders get stuck believing "who you are" is fixed. They believe they're hopelessly trapped in a cycle of perpetually attracting the wrong thing, given their past and current limitations, fears, or people-pleasing patterns.

The Productivity Paradox in Leadership

I see this paradox every day in my consulting and coaching practice. Brilliant executives working 70-hour weeks but making no progress on goals that align with their authentic mission. Leaders drowning in productivity tools while feeling less effective.

Alex, a director of operations at a Fortune 500 company came to me with 23 active projects and zero completed strategic initiatives. He had color-coded spreadsheets, premium productivity apps, and a schedule packed tighter than a Tetris game.

"I'm maximizing every minute," he told me proudly, showing me his optimized calendar. But when I asked about his quarterly goal—launching a new operational framework that could save the company millions—he paused. "Well, I haven't been able to focus on that. Too many urgent priorities."

Alex wasn't lazy or unfocused. He was trapped in productivity theater, looking incredibly busy while making zero progress on what mattered most. The transformation happened when we applied (**Strengths + Core Values + Mission**) × **Emotional Recognition = Your Authentic Imprint.** We discovered that Alex's strength in systems thinking was being scattered across 23 random projects instead of focused on the one strategic initiative that aligned with his authentic mission. Armed with this new understanding of himself, he completed his strategic framework and implemented it within 90 days, saving the company $2.3M annually. Alex felt energized instead of exhausted because his work finally aligned with his authentic purpose.

When the four elements of Your Authentic Imprint align, productivity becomes natural rather than forced. Work energizes you instead of draining you. Too many high-performing leaders are stuck in a cycle of back-to-back meetings, endless tasks, and constant motion—yet making little real progress toward their most meaningful goals.

If you're busy looking busy, but accomplishing little that matters, try conducting an Authentic Goal Audit as a starting point for a much-needed revolution in your productivity:

- List your current projects or tasks that you want to accomplish.
- Circle the ones that energize you.
- Cross out the ones that drain you. The ones that drained you were most likely activities not aligned with your unique talents.
- Now, choose the single most important goal that aligns with your authentic mission and give it your peak energy this week.

You were not created to pursue objectives that don't align with your authentic purpose. You were made for a mission that is uniquely yours. When you operate from your personal mission mindset, your energy soars.

The Neuroscience of Scattered Leadership

The average executive checks email every 6 minutes, switches between applications over 1,100 times per day, and experiences an interruption every 11 minutes. Translate that to the home environment and you realize that we're living through what researchers call "the attention apocalypse." It's costing organizations their competitive edge, their innovation capacity, and their best talent. It's taxing individuals much more than that. The average human attention span has shrunk to 8 seconds or less, and it takes an average of 23 minutes to refocus after an interruption. When your attention is constantly fragmented, you lose access to what neuroscientists call "the executive network"—the brain circuits responsible for strategic thinking, creative problem-solving, and wise decision-making.

Consider Jamie, Marketing Director at a fast-growing startup, who prided herself on being instantly responsive. She had Slack notifications enabled, email pushed to her phone, and maintained an open-door policy for her team of 12.

"I'm completely accessible," she told me. "My team never has to wait for answers."

But here's what Jamie didn't realize: Her constant availability was destroying her ability to think strategically. She hadn't completed a single deep analysis or innovative campaign in four months. Her team was getting quick answers to tactical questions but missing out on the strategic leadership they needed.

The wake-up call came during a quarterly review when her CEO asked about the new market expansion strategy Jamie was supposed to be developing. She had started it dozens of times but never had more than 20 minutes of uninterrupted thinking.

We then implemented what I call "Strategic Sanctuary" time—protected blocks where Jamie was completely unavailable for anything except her most important thinking work. Inspired by this simple change to her schedule, Jamie developed a market expansion strategy that resulted in 40% revenue growth in the targeted segment. Her team reported feeling more confident because they were getting higher-quality strategic direction, not just quick tactical responses.

If your mind is constantly fragmented, your decision-making ability is seriously hampered. We can forget trying to be superhuman in the age of constant distraction because research shows that decision-making uses a finite mental resource. Every choice you make—from what to wear to which strategic direction to pursue—depletes the same cognitive tank. Decision fatigue is real. A 2024 McKinsey & Company study found that companies with leaders who successfully learned to handle decision fatigue saw an interesting result—they outperformed their peers by 22% in profitability over a five-year period.[26]

Consider Maya, founder of a rapidly growing fintech startup, who was drowning in decisions while trying to build a productive culture. Every day brought hundreds of choices: hiring decisions, product features, customer issues, vendor selections, team conflicts, and strategic pivots.

"I'm making decisions all day," she told me. "But by afternoon, I can't think clearly about the big choices that could make or break our company."

Maya's team was mirroring her scattered decision-making. They would bring every small choice to her rather than take ownership. The culture had become one of learned helplessness, where everyone waited for Maya's approval on everything.

Meanwhile, Maya was making increasingly poor strategic choices as her decision fatigue mounted throughout each day. She would agree to partnerships she later regretted, hire people who weren't quite right, and change product direction based on the last customer conversation she'd had.

There are practical exercises, like finding your Focus Window where you identify your most mentally sharp 90-minute period daily and protect it fiercely. You likely know to create interruption-free zones where you turn off notifications and put your phone in another room. But there is an even more radical notion regarding improving your productivity. Neuroscience research reveals that our brains operate on natural energy rhythms. When we work within these patterns on goals that align with our authentic purpose, then our cognitive performance soars. When we work against these patterns, everything (including making key decisions) becomes exponentially harder. The key insight here? Human beings aren't machines. We have natural energy rhythms and wiring that, when honored, dramatically improve performance and satisfaction.

It all comes back to one thing. You don't need to be more productive—you need to be more you—and live and lead from that fundamental truth.

Cracking Your Love Code

When you start attracting from love instead of fear, from authenticity instead of performance, everything shifts. You attract team members who want to do their best work, not just collect paychecks. You attract opportunities that align with your mission, not just your ambition. You attract challenges that grow you, not just stress you.

The following five exercises can help you crack the love code and open the door to future possibilities and more productivity that counts.

1. **Take the Authentic Imprint Assessment:** If you haven't already done so, you can go online at danawilliamsco.scoreapp.com and take the free 3-minute Authentic Imprint Assessment. You can discover your authentic leadership profile and get your personalized roadmap for making a greater impact. It is one of the easiest ways you can honestly evaluate where you're operating from authenticity, versus strictly performance.

2. **Start a journaling practice:** Commit to five minutes each morning and evening for practicing the daily work of self-love and pursuing authentic alignment with what's most important.

3. **Identify your people-pleasing patterns:** Where are you still reacting to others instead of responding from love? What would change if you operated from deep security instead of desperate approval?

4. **Practice the oxygen mask principle:** What is one way you can love yourself better this week? How can you put

on your own mask first before helping others? Fill your own tank so that you can serve from overflow.

5. **Trust your heart:** What is your heart telling you about your authentic path that your mind has been arguing against? What would L-O-V-E do?

Remember, you attract who you are, not what you want. But when you learn to love who you authentically are—when you crack your own love code—you start attracting exactly what you want. You draw opportunities that fit, teams that thrive, and the kind of success that feels as good as it looks. The Internal Revolution starts within, surrounded by love.

Looking Ahead

How well do you communicate about your authentic personal brand? In this next chapter, you will learn the pitfalls to avoid and strategies to implement when communicating about Your Authentic Imprint. Courageously conveying who you know yourself to be—and protecting that authentic self by setting healthy boundaries (despite the risk of disappointing some people)—will help you succeed in the Internal Revolution.

∾

Worth Remembering:
Every day, you get to choose: Will you live in default mode, letting old patterns run your responses? Or will you design your day through micro-moments of authentic choice? Your daily Internal Revolution starts with one conscious choice at a time.

PUTTING IT INTO PRACTICE

QUESTIONS FOR REFLECTION

1. How do you define productivity?
2. What needless pressure do you tend to put on yourself?
3. Why do you think you do that?
4. How can you be truly productive this week?

EXERCISE 1

As part of your new understanding of productivity, practice using the following three tools every day to Dominate Your Day this week.

> **The Breath Revolution (30 seconds)**
> Take three deep breaths and ask: "What would my strongest self do right now?" Let your top strengths guide your response instead of your old habits.

> **The Question Revolution (1-2 minutes)**
> Ask, "Why am I feeling this way? What old story is this activating?" Then consciously choose: "What story do I want to live instead?"

> **The Affirmation Revolution (2-3 minutes)**
> Speak your strengths directly to the situation using your Strengths Affirmation from chapter 2.

EXERCISE 2

Practice True, Tune, Turn this week—a simple yet powerful three-step decision-making framework designed to help you make choices while planning your day that fully align with your unique strengths, core values, and mission. In other words, Your Authentic Imprint.

- **True:** When an opportunity or decision perfectly reflects your authentic strengths and values, it's a clear "go." This is where you act decisively and confidently, knowing it supports your mission and emotional clarity.
- **Tune:** Sometimes, an option has potential but needs refinement or adjustment to better align with Your Authentic Imprint. This step invites you to thoughtfully tweak, develop, or gather more information before moving forward.
- **Turn:** If a choice fundamentally conflicts with your core values or mission, it's time to say "no" and turn away. This empowers you to protect your authenticity and focus your energy where it truly matters.

By using **True, Tune, Turn**, you create space for intentional, values-driven decisions that honor who you are and where you want to go—ensuring every step you take leaves a meaningful, Authentic Imprint.

Scan to order The Strengths Journal.
thestrengthsjournal.com

PART 3

Transform Your Life

CHAPTER 7

Protecting Your Authentic Imprint: Better Communication and Boundaries

When someone mentions "personal branding," what's the first thing most people think of? Let me guess. A LinkedIn influencer posting their morning routine with a motivational quote? That colleague who seems to have turned themselves into a walking, talking elevator pitch? If you're like most of the leaders I work with, you may think: "That's not me. I don't want to be that person."

Here's the thing—you're absolutely right. That's not you. And thank goodness.

Still, Harvard Business Review and other leadership research consistently reveal a troubling disconnect: many executives avoid working on their personal brand because it feels "inauthentic" or "self-promotional." Yet the same research shows that leaders who develop authentic personal brands rooted in their true values and strengths are more likely to advance in their careers and more effective at attracting and retaining top talent. The disconnect? Most personal branding advice focuses on "packaging" leaders like products, rather than helping them authentically communicate their personal and unique value and meaningful contribution to this world.

Sarah, a vice president of operations at a tech company, spent six months trying to build her "personal brand" using traditional advice. She diligently studied successful executives in her industry, copied their content style, and posted motivational quotes that sounded nothing like how she talked in real life.

"I was getting engagement," she told me, "but it felt completely fake. I didn't recognize myself in what I was posting." Sarah's breaking point came when a colleague said, "I saw your post about resilience, but it didn't sound like you at all. Are you okay?"

The problem wasn't Sarah's content strategy. It was a communication strategy error. She was trying to build someone else's brand instead of expressing the nuances of her own authentic leadership. She was so ready to pursue her Authentic Imprint instead.

Better Communication of Who You Are

Transformation happened for Sarah when we applied the formula for intentional daily living: (**Strengths + Core Values + Mission**) × **Emotional Recognition** = **Your Authentic Imprint**. As we unpacked these elements one by one, we discovered Sarah's key strengths in systems thinking and her top core value of inclusive leadership.

Instead of posting generic inspiration, she improved her communication with her audience by sharing intriguing insights about what mattered most to her. She talked about building operational systems that supported people, not just processes. Consequently, Sarah's engagement increased 50%. More important, she started attracting opportunities that aligned with her authentic mission. Three senior executives reached out about positions that specifically required her unique combination of operational excellence and people-first leadership. In other words, they were drawn to the "real Sarah."

Communicating in a Real Way

Your personal brand isn't what you do; it's who you are when you're doing it. When your brand flows from the real you, something magical happens. You stop attracting just "any" opportunities and start attracting the right opportunities.

Maybe you need a reminder right about now to stop trying to be impressive. Instead, recall that you are the one-and-only you on the planet, which inherently makes you invaluable—sans any kind of performance. The world has enough people trying to be impressive. What it needs are people of influence who are brave enough to become uniquely irreplaceable.

This week, I encourage you to conduct a Brand Honesty Audit. Look at your current professional and personal online presence. Does what you're communicating sound/look like the real you? Or does it just sound and look like who you think you should be? Why or why not?

The next challenge is an Authentic Expression Experiment. This is where you take week or so and share one perspective that's genuinely yours, instead of what you think people want to hear. You can do this online or in person, using any format you choose. Afterward, reflect on what you learned about yourself. How did it feel to speak from the heart? What was the response?

Authenticity Takes Time

Sometimes the most authentic thing you can do is wait. While planning ahead for an upcoming vacation, I intended to write a post for July 4th—something about family vacation, gratitude, maybe a sunset photo from Turks and Caicos. The kind of content we often think we're supposed to share.

But then tragedy struck close to home, and suddenly that planned post felt hollow. Empty. Performative. On June 26, 2025, my granddaughter returned from Camp Mystic in South Texas. On the morning of July 4 a few days later, we learned that several young campers and their beloved camp director at the same camp had lost their lives in flooding on the Guadalupe River.

Our family—like so many others—began processing the grief amid gratitude that our granddaughter was safe. We had to wade through the complicated emotions that come when tragedy touches your world.

I didn't post anything for July 4. Instead, I waited.

I've learned something about authentic communication. Sometimes the most genuine response is admitting you don't know how you feel yet. As leaders, we often feel pressure to have the right words immediately. To post something meaningful. To show up perfectly composed. But real leadership sometimes looks like saying, "I need time to process this. I'm not ready to speak yet."

My thoughts kept returning to a simple children's book we'd been reading together with my granddaughters called *Waiting is Not Easy*. It became my gentle reminder that some of life's most important moments require patience—even when everything in me wants to act, speak, or post immediately.

Not every holiday needs a post. Not every moment needs to be shared. Not every season requires performance. The world has enough people trying to say the right thing quickly. What it needs are people brave enough to take time, to feel deeply, and then speak authentically when they're ready. Your people don't need you to be impressive. They need you to be real.

The Authenticity Trap—
Why "Just Be Yourself" Isn't Enough

"Just be yourself." It's the most common advice in personal branding. It's also completely useless. Why? Because most leaders have spent so many years being who they thought they should be that they've lost touch with who they are. You can't "just be yourself," if you don't know what that means anymore. This was me for so many years in the corporate workspace.

The result? Leaders either avoid personal branding entirely (like I did) or create artificial versions of authenticity that feel just as performative as the traditional approach. Harvard Business Review researcher Herminia Ibarra even discovered an "authenticity paradox" that trips up even the most self-aware leaders.[27] According to her findings, striving for authenticity is harder than it appears and can sometimes unintentionally create the opposite effect. When you rigidly cling to a fixed idea of who you are, you limit your growth and effectiveness. But when you try too hard to be authentic in every situation, it starts to feel forced and unnatural. It's like being caught between two bad options. Traditional branding feels fake, but self-conscious attempts at authenticity feel just as, well, inauthentic.

You end up either performing someone else's version of leadership or performing your own guess at who you should be—and both are exhausting. The real issue? Most people are trying to be authentic without first doing the internal work to understand what their authentic self looks like beneath all the professional and social conditioning. They can't communicate effectively about the core of who they are because they honestly don't know.

We've all had moments where our actions don't align with who we say we are—sometimes without realizing it. I once interviewed someone for a possible speaking role on a panel. Their bio highlighted expertise in personal branding, and their story aligned beautifully with the theme we wanted to showcase—authenticity. On paper, they seemed like the perfect fit. In person, their presence didn't match their profile.

The confidence and passion I expected from their bio came across flat in conversation. Their body language was closed off, they avoided eye contact, and their answers sounded rehearsed. The energy and authenticity they described in writing didn't carry through in real time. It was a reminder to me—and to all of us—that authenticity isn't just about the story we tell. It's about showing up consistently so that our message and our presence are aligned. When we are living authentically both online and offline, it doesn't feel "off." We don't have to perform or "copy and paste" a version of ourselves. What a relief to simply be who we truly are.

When Being Yourself Doesn't Feel Right

Consider Michael, a senior director at a Fortune 500 company, who decided to "be more authentic" after attending a traditional personal branding workshop. He started posting and sharing more personal stories and opinions, but something still felt off.

"I'm being more myself," he told me, "but it still doesn't feel right. I'm sharing personal stuff, but it feels as if I'm performing authenticity instead of just being authentic."

Like Sarah, Michael's problem wasn't his content—it was that he was trying to be authentic without first understanding what his authentic self looked like in a professional context. We dug deeper using the Authentic Imprint Assessment he completed online to reveal unique angles of his particular leadership style, areas where he could grow, and next steps. Michael discovered that his attempts at authenticity were expressing his people-pleasing patterns (wanting to be liked) rather than his authentic leadership strengths (strategic thinking and direct communication).

Once Michael understood his actual Authentic Imprint—the real Michael began to show through. What transformed his professional presence involved his recognizing and naming his unique combination of analytical strengths + integrity-based values + his passion for his mission to solve complex business problems.

Instead of sharing personal stories to "seem" relatable, Michael began sharing his unique analytical perspectives on industry challenges. He knew this aspect of the field by heart, and his content became genuinely helpful, rather than just personally revealing. Senior executives started reaching out for his insights, and he was promoted within eight months.

Let's go back to our definition: **Your Authentic Imprint is the unmistakable energy and authenticity you bring—whether in person or online—the living, breathing impression you leave on others, day after day. It's not about being more impressive, but about being more you.**

Michael was finally recognized as the expert in his field that he always was. But it was authenticity that opened the way for better communication with his audience. And better communication brought the accolades, recognition, and opportunities. Your authenticity is your authority—but only when you know what authenticity means for you. An authentic leader is powerful at home and at work because he or she is truly comfortable communicating in his or her own skin.

Better Communication in Three Steps

The goal of better communication, as it relates to personal branding, isn't to share more about yourself and make others uncomfortable—it's to express more of yourself and make an impact. So how do you get there?

Authentic personal branding that taps into the "real you" can be broken down into three simple steps. In fact, the process makes so much common sense that you'll wonder why you didn't discover it earlier.

> **Step One Discovery** – Understanding your actual Authentic Imprint (not who you think you should be)

Step Two Alignment – Ensuring your professional and personal expression matches your authentic core

Step Three Integration – Bringing your authentic self to the way you influence others while maintaining personal integrity and without losing professionalism at work

You can apply these three steps in your personal life with family and friends just as easily as you can apply them in your work life. In fact, if you don't employ these three steps in both worlds, I predict you might come down with a serious case of impostor syndrome in one or both areas! The rest of this chapter will help you process these simple steps. Part 3 Transform Your Life is aptly named because this is where you have a chance to step out into a whole new future.

Core Practice Experiment

Let me ask you something. When you're "being" authentic, are you expressing your true strengths and values, or are you just attempting to be more personal to no effect? How do you know which one is the case? One way to find out is through a Core Practice Experiment. Here, you identify one of your top core identities (built on strengths and/or core values) that you rarely express professionally or personally—but you feel this way deep in your soul. Find one small way this week to let that closely held identity show. The goal isn't to share more about yourself—it's to express more of your real self. After you complete the experiment, reflect on what you learned.

I love dreaming up new frameworks, visuals, and possibilities (honestly, it's a top strength and my happy place). However, when I was in my corporate role back in the day, it dawned on me that I was not drawing on this strength at work. Why wasn't I letting it shine in my leadership meetings? After reflecting on the problem, I realized that I'd convinced myself that I needed to keep things practical and polished in order to be "taken seriously" among my peers. At the same time that I buried my top strength I also downplayed one of my core values—stepping outside of the box. I was playing it safe instead of playing it real.

So I ran a Core Practice Experiment. I picked one of my upcoming team sessions to introduce a new, creative framework I'd been thinking about, even though the idea wasn't fully finished. I used a visual sketch (think back-of-the-napkin-meets-brand-strategy) and shared the concept as a conversation starter. Guess what happened? Instead of judgment, I got engagement. People leaned in. They added ideas. They got excited. I felt energized, not exposed. That one moment led to a new workshop format we now use regularly in my business.

My ability to come up with new ideas rose to the surface, along with my core value of innovation. When I allowed those two to take the wheel—just for a moment—I didn't lose excellence or credibility. I gained connection. It was a reminder that bringing more of your true self to bear is often the very thing you and the people you're trying to influence needs most of all.

The Comparison Game—How Other People's Success Is Killing Your Authentic Brand

Of all the ways we muddy how we communicate about ourselves, the comparison game is the fastest way to destroy an authentic personal brand. When you're constantly measuring your presence against others, especially in a professional sense, you stop expressing who you are and start trying to become who they are instead.

> "Their post got so many comments. Mine got 12."
> "They speak at all the big conferences. I've never been invited to anything."
> "Everyone seems to have it all figured out in life except me."

Sound familiar?

Comparison is not just a bad idea—it carries with it a physical consequence. Psychology research tells us that when you're constantly measuring yourself against others, your brain gets stuck in a stress cycle that makes it harder to think strategically or solve problems creatively. It's like trying to do your best work while someone's constantly tapping you on the shoulder asking, "But what about them? What about what they're doing?"

Executives, employees, moms and dads, college graduates taking their first job, newlyweds buying their first home, retirees figuring out what to do with their day—no one is an exception to this phenomenon. Psychologists have a term for this constant external validation-seeking: "comparison stress." It's stressful because of the mental fatigue that comes from always looking sideways at others instead of forward.

But here's the really insidious part: When you're building your brand based on what's working for other people, you naturally progress to the next step in your own demise. You start wanting what they have or what they do, instead of pursuing what aligns with your authentic mission that you are called and equipped to accomplish in this lifetime. Social psychologists call it "mimetic desire" where you start copying other people's dreams, instead of following your own.

Case in point. Jessica was a marketing director who became obsessed with building the kind of personal brand she saw other leaders achieving. She carefully watched how successful executives posted online, noted which topics got the most engagement, and started crafting content that by all accounts was designed to go viral.

"I was spending hours analyzing what worked for others," she confessed. "I had spreadsheets tracking the best posting times, the most engaging content types, the hashtags that drove traffic." Jessica's metrics improved with this artificial framework, but something crucial was missing. Despite growing followers and engagement, she wasn't attracting the right opportunities that were significant to her. She was getting noticed, but not for anything that mattered to her unique authentic mission (that, by the way, had nothing to do with the content she was posting).

The wake-up call came when the impostor she pretended to be online received three job interviews—all for roles that would have been a step backward in terms of the work she wanted to do. How did this happen? She had never communicated anything from the real Jessica. Her comparison-driven brand was attracting attention, but not the right kind that suited her!

First, I challenged her to stop asking, "What works for

others?" and begin asking, "What can my authentic self contribute?" Sometimes this question leads to a deer in the headlights kind of prolonged silence, like someone who has no idea who they are or the contribution they can make.

I am no longer surprised by this blank response, because the damage we've allowed to our own self-confidence and God-given gifts is real. But it does serve as a reminder that the Internal Revolution entails a deep dive into patterns and our past—and a willingness to work on our stuff. Inner work is difficult work that many people don't want to do.

However, Jessica dove right in it. Through effort and over time, she discovered her underlying unique combination of creative strategy and data-driven execution. Those were her real strengths, so what could she do with them? Instead of copying industry thought leaders, she began communicating her own frameworks for balancing creativity with measurable results. Jessica's engagement remained strong, but the quality of opportunities that came her way dramatically improved. Most important, she felt energized by her professional presence, instead of exhausted by Imposter Syndrome.

Breaking Free from the Comparison Trap

If you want to communicate better about who you are at your core, it's time for a Comparison Inventory. Notice when you find yourself comparing yourself to others this week. What triggers it? To whom do you compare yourself most? Why is that? Consider how you tend to compare yourself to others in a personal sense—and also how you might compare your professional presence.

Follow up those insights with another exercise I call Unique Value Identification. Write down three positive things you bring to the table. Note what you contribute as a friend, a daughter or son, a spouse, or a parent that no one else brings in quite the same way. Remind yourself what you bring to leadership at work that nobody else in your network brings in quite the same way. Get detailed.

The antidote to comparison isn't avoiding other successful leaders—it's becoming so clear on your own Authentic Imprint that external success stories inspire rather than intimidate you. When you know who you are and what you're uniquely positioned to contribute, other people's success becomes data points rather than judgment points.

There is room for everyone's authentic contribution. Your irreplaceable brand isn't about being better than others; it's about being the one and only you. And that's more than enough.

The world doesn't need another version of someone else—it needs the original version of the real you. Communicate who that person is exceptionally well, and you're halfway there to protecting your authentic brand.

Setting proper boundaries is the other half of protecting the your authentic self, and we'll unpack that concept next. Boundaries and communication go hand in hand when you're serious about wanting to transform your life. Getting better at sharing who you know yourself to be—and protecting that authentic self with healthy boundaries—are dual priorities for those of us in the trenches of the Internal Revolution. Let's explore boundary setting in a way that you may not have thought about before.

Setting Boundaries That Protect Your Authentic Brand (Without Burning Bridges)

Jason habitually prioritized the needs and desires of others over his own. He put himself last on the list, always responding to what others wanted from him no matter what time it was or how much he needed someone to pay attention to his needs. Someone needed a loan? Jason put himself in debt before he would tell someone no. Volunteers were needed at a community event? Sign him up. If his boss emailed him after hours, Jason responded immediately because he believed doing so was his only option. When he was frustrated with a friend or relationship, nobody could even tell because Jason always avoided conflict and kept his thoughts to himself.

Then there's David, a regional sales director who prided himself on being the most responsive leader in his organization. He answered emails within minutes, said yes to every meeting request, and never shared opinions that might create waves.

"I want to be known as someone people can count on," he told me. "I'm building my brand as the reliable, agreeable leader."

But David's brand was undermining his leadership. By saying yes to everything, he was saying no to his authentic strengths in strategic thinking. By avoiding his real opinions, he was robbing his team of the insights they needed.

Jason, the people-pleasing friend, and David, the always available executive, illustrate those of us whose mantras fall along the lines of:

"I say yes to everything because I want to be seen as a team player."

"I never share my real opinions because I don't want to ruffle feathers."
"I'm available 24/7 because that's what good leaders do."

If any of these confessions sound familiar, I have to say you're in good company. I've been there myself. Consequently, I can say with certainty that in those moments you're not building an authentic personal brand—you're building a people-pleasing prison. The most influential and relatable people don't say "yes" to everything. Rather, their personal brand is built on having the courage to say "no" to what doesn't align with who they are and "yes" to what does.

You see, once you know who you are and can communicate that clearly and effectively with ease, you'll want to protect that revelation with all your might. Leadership research consistently shows that authenticity and clear boundaries are foundational to effective leadership.[28] In fact, when leaders regularly operate outside of their core strengths and values, they experience the kind of chronic stress that impacts decision-making quality and creative thinking.

Research in various fields like occupational health and psychology support this truth, indicating that abandoning ourselves also leads to a cascade of other problems— including reduced job satisfaction.[29] In other words, if you no longer love your job, there's a reason; and the consequences are real. Meanwhile, additional studies on authentic leadership demonstrate that leaders who maintain boundaries that protect their core values and strengths report significantly higher job satisfaction and more effective team performance.[30]

Your authentic brand is protected by what you don't do as

much as what you do. I often advocate that clients who struggle with healthy boundaries conduct a Boundary Audit, starting by identifying one area where their lack of boundaries is undermining their authentic leadership. Ask yourself, "What are you saying yes to that you should be saying no to?

> **Your Revolution** – Choose one small boundary in either a professional or personal context to implement this week. Start with something low risk but meaningful to your authentic expression.

The goal isn't to become difficult in your relationships with others—it's to become clear about who you are and what you stand for. Effective boundaries aren't about keeping people out as much as they're about keeping yourself aligned. After all, your personal brand isn't built in isolation—it's forged in community. Our relationships with others affect our leadership and our decisions more than we often realize. Choose relationships that reflect not only who you are but also who you're becoming.

Boundary Framework for Authentic Leaders

Something tells me that you haven't done all this inner work so far in chapters 1-6 to lose momentum now. So what kind of boundaries are we talking about? I see four key areas of your authentic self to protect:

> **Communication Boundaries:** Sharing your genuine perspective while maintaining professional respect and personal integrity

Energy Boundaries: Protecting your time and attention for what energizes your authentic contribution

Mission Boundaries: Saying no to opportunities that don't serve your authentic purpose

Value Boundaries: Making decisions that align with your core values, even when it's uncomfortable to do so

The first one, Communication Boundaries, we've already addressed in this chapter. The last one, Value Boundaries, is something I want to explore more thoroughly because making small and large decisions based on your core values affects all three boundaries around your mission, around your energy, and around your daily communication.

Value-Based Boundaries
Making Decisions That Matter Most

When President John F. Kennedy made the audacious decision to put a man on the moon, he wasn't choosing the easy path. He wasn't seeking consensus or trying to please everyone in Congress. He made a decision that aligned with his vision of America's potential, a bold choice that would transform not only the space program but also America's entire sense of what was possible.

Today's leaders face a crisis of authenticity in decision-making—many times because they lack boundary clarity on their own deeply-held core values. In our hyperconnected, consensus-seeking workplace culture, we've created a generation of leaders paralyzed by the need for harmony, trapped by people-pleasing tendencies, and disconnected from their authentic decision-making power. The uncomfortable truth is that you are limiting yourself every day that you avoid the decisions that matter most.

- Are you avoiding decisions that might displease people?
- Are you seeking consensus instead of creating direction?
- Are you going after things you already know how to get?
- Are you playing it safe when bold choices are needed?

Before you can make powerful decisions, you must ask yourself the fundamental question: Am I being completely honest with myself? Authentic decision-making starts with brutal self-awareness.

The Authentic Decision-Making Process

Most decision-making frameworks ignore the reality that we all think and process differently. In other words, they leave out the key role our strengths play in our decisions. What you want is an approach to decision-making that honors your unique strengths and authentic self.

Start by reflecting on an area in your personal or professional life where a boundary would not only enhance your wellbeing or productivity but also allow you to make decisions that resonate with who you are at your core. By leveraging your strengths in this situation, you can begin to communicate these boundaries effectively and respectfully, using what you learn in this chapter.

Now, leverage what you've learned so far about your strengths. The challenge is to use your unique strengths to establish boundaries. For example, if your strengths revolve around creating structure and order (Executing), consider how you might need better boundaries protecting your time—and then make decisions accordingly. If your strengths lie in your ability to build connections (Relationship Building), it will be important to you to set boundaries by seeking mutually beneficial solutions. Your decisions would then follow suit.

In Chapter 6, you learned True, Tune, Turn—a quick filter for daily choices. Now, when the stakes are higher, try the following Authentic Decision-Making Process. These 7 steps can help you build on your strengths and decide with confidence:

1. Clarify the Real Choice

Strip away the noise, politics, and emotions. What is the actual decision that needs to be made? Not the symptoms or side issues—name the core choice at hand.

2. Seek Truth, Not Confirmation

Gather perspectives and data, but resist the urge to only collect information that supports what you already want to do. You rarely have to sell yourself on a truly good idea.

3. Expand Your Options

Turn up your creative and strategic thinking. What possibilities exist beyond the obvious binary choice? Challenge yourself to find a third way for consideration.

4. Apply the Regret Minimization Test

This framework, memorably used by Jeff Bezos when deciding to leave his lucrative Wall Street job to start Amazon, is powerful in its simplicity. Ask yourself: "On a scale of 1-10, how much would I regret this decision if it doesn't work out?" Now flip it and ask: "How much would I regret not making this decision?" Make your time horizon for this decision the next one to three years.

5. Decide from Your Core Values

Make the choice that aligns with your authentic self and creates the greatest potential for impact. Trust your strengths and values, not the crowd.

6. Execute with Purpose

Remember that the pain of executing your decision today creates the success of tomorrow.

7. Reflect and Evolve

Every decision becomes wisdom for your next choice. What did you learn about yourself, your process, and your impact by making this decision?

The Daily Practice

Powerful decision-making isn't just about the big moments—it's about building authentic decision-making as a daily habit. Consider these five practices:

1. **Know Your Talents:** Understand your strengths and how they show up in decision-making.

2. **Daily Check-ins:** Ask yourself each morning, "What decision am I avoiding today?"
3. **Better Daily Decisions = Better Outcomes:** Practice on small decisions to build your decision-making muscle.
4. **Plan with Intention:** Align your choices with your core values and vision.
5. **Be Consistent:** Make authenticity your default, not your exception.

The Courage to Choose

Courage doesn't always feel good, does it? Making the right decision and setting boundaries often means disappointing people in the short term to serve them better in the long term. It means having the difficult conversations and choosing direction over popularity.

My encouragement to you is to stop going after things you already know how to get. Stop limiting yourself with the need for universal approval. Your organization, your team, your family, and all those closest to you rely on you to express who you really are consistently, set clear boundaries, and lead forward from your authentic core. The Internal Revolution isn't happening in the boardroom or the ballot box—it's happening in the mirror, in the daily choices that either move you toward your authentic potential or keep you playing small.

Looking Ahead

If the predictions about the scale of AI are accurate, in the near future we will all be working with and interacting more with robots and humans interchangeably. The time is now to clarify your personal brand (Your Authentic Imprint) and ensure human to human interaction remains strong. In this final chapter, we're focusing on a skill that's more valuable than ever in our digital world: building authentic connections. In a screen-driven culture and workplace, the ability to form genuine and mutually beneficial relationships is essential. You were never meant to complete the Internal Revolution alone.

∼

Worth Remembering:
The best leaders and most influential people among us live the way they've always wanted to live. They aren't lucky—they're decisive. They understand that life is not just about choosing between options; it's about choosing and crafting and protecting who you become.

PUTTING IT INTO PRACTICE

QUESTIONS FOR REFLECTION

1. What decisions do you tend to put off?
2. Where are you communicating from your core most effectively?
3. What boundary do you have trouble establishing?
4. How do you define having the courage to do what you must do?

EXERCISE 1

Your action items for this week:
- Identify one decision you've been avoiding because it might displease people
- Complete the regret minimization exercise for that decision
- Leverage your top strengths to create a clear path forward
- Make the decision, and communicate it with authenticity and conviction
- What boundary can you set to protect that decision?

EXERCISE 2

If you take time to reflect, you evolve. Every decision becomes wisdom for your next choice. What did you learn about yourself, your process, and your impact in Exercise 1?

CHAPTER 8

The Secret of Connection: Community Makes it Work

From living in his car and battling addiction to becoming a director at a men's recovery center in Texas, Rand's transformation shows how tapping into your innate strengths can reshape not just a career, but an entire life.

When we began working together one year ago, Rand's strengths were evident, but not yet fully activated. Early on, I noticed he lacked the structure that his strengths in self-discipline needed to thrive in his expanding leadership role. Studying strengths alignment for so many years has taught me that the solutions to most of our problems are already inside of us. When I encouraged him to apply his strengths in problem-solving and fixing things inward and create weekly planning routines, things began to shift. Previously, Rand had used that strength to solve others' problems and to help them heal, but he hadn't turned that same power inward. Once he did, his personal growth accelerated, but something was still missing.

In a later session, he revealed that he felt most motivated when he could measure his progress. That insight unlocked his need to engage his competitiveness, another strength, with clear benchmarks. Together, we created a leadership plan with specific objectives, giving him a tangible way to see growth.

I saw the impact firsthand at a Christmas event where Rand led worship with confidence and authenticity. Later, his leader sent me a video of him speaking at a prominent Dallas church—more evidence of his transformation. He told me afterward that sharing his story was hard, but he absolutely loved the experience (a big sign his strengths were at work).

His next breakthrough came six months later with his promotion to Director. Like every leader, Rand continues to grow. Old habits resurface like comparing himself to others, doubting his uniqueness. He now participates in a leadership program with peers who push him to aim higher. As he said in our latest session, "Having others just a few steps ahead of me gives me something to aim for. I finally understand how to harness what drives me."

If I didn't see it with my own eyes, I might not believe that a fractured young man could heal his own wounds and emerge stronger than ever before. His combination of strengths offered the perfect foundation for transformation, once Rand leveraged his unique wiring to power his goals. Rand's strengths had never left him; they had just been overshadowed for years by his disadvantages and weakness. While the adage suggests people should "work on their weaknesses," I'm a firm believer in decades of Gallup research that has demonstrated the opposite. It may sound counter-intuitive, but focusing on one's strengths instead like Rand did leads to greater engagement, productivity, and success.

Most important in Rand's transformative journey is the fact that he didn't do it alone—an entire community of accountability and encouragement surrounded him and shored him up in the difficult times, solidifying his positive choices and changes so that he could one day help change others forever. Community and connection are the last crucial elements we need to explore in the process of the Internal Revolution.

> **Your Revolution** – Which of your natural strengths might be misdirected or underutilized? What would change if you intentionally redirected that strength toward an area where you're seeking growth? Who will help you get there?

From Performance to Presence

Let me tell you about Lisa, CEO of a 500-person manufacturing company, who had built her entire leadership brand on being the "perfect" executive. She had the right words for every situation, the polished presentation for every board meeting, and the carefully crafted response for every challenge.

"I've got leadership 'figured out,'" she told me. "I know exactly how to show up in every situation."

But Lisa's perfect performance soon created an unexpected problem. Her team had stopped bringing her real problems because they felt they needed to have perfect solutions before approaching her. Innovation had stagnated because everyone was afraid to share half-formed ideas.

The wake-up call came when her head of product told her, "We respect you, but we don't feel like we know you. And if we don't know you, how can we really follow you?"

Lisa realized her performance-based brand, while impressive, had created distance instead of connection on her team, empty compliance instead of commitment. She had accidentally become the bottleneck she was trying to eliminate! By always providing solutions, she was preventing others from developing their own problem-solving capabilities.

The plot twist came in our work together when Lisa discovered that coming up with the answers herself for her team and co-workers wasn't her real strength at all. In fact, her attempt to have it all together all the time was taking its toll on her personally. Following her Authentic Imprint, Lisa realized that what she really enjoyed and excelled at doing involved asking the right questions to help others find and contribute to great breakthrough solutions. Everything changed when she discovered the power of strategic questions.

Instead of reviewing David's proposal and giving feedback, Lisa scheduled a 15-minute conversation and asked: "Walk me through your thinking process on this. What criteria are you using to make these decisions?"

The next time someone else on the team brought her a problem, before she offered solutions she asked: "What approaches have you already considered? What would you do if you had to solve this independently?" When she saw someone second-guessing good thinking, she wanted to know: "What's making you doubt that approach?"

Lisa opened up and shared with others about her thought process as they worked through complex problems together. Suddenly, teams felt safe sharing incomplete ideas in search of better ones.

Thoughtful questions don't just solve problems—they build problem-solvers. The goal was no longer to have all the answers; it became asking good questions that unlocked the answers her team was capable of sharing. Instead of showing up with polished presentations, Lisa became genuinely curious about her team's strengths. Instead of presenting the right response to every challenge herself, she started bringing others in.

The greatest leadership opportunity isn't providing all the answers—because let's be honest, you don't have them all! It's creating clarity within chaos. This is where understanding your natural talents becomes such a powerful advantage. When you lead from your authentic strengths, rather than trying to become someone you're not, you create steadiness that others can feel and follow.

At Lisa's company, innovation metrics increased 15% within six months and employee engagement scores reached all-time highs, driving unprecedented collaboration across departments. Her company changed—not only because Lisa changed, but also because her team helped facilitate and complete her personal transformation.

The Context Is Community

None of the principles I teach in this book about strengths and Your Authentic Imprint work in isolation—only within the context of community. This is one of the main differences between performance-based leadership and presence-based leadership.

A "performance" is something you can do all by yourself, like a soliloquy at a play. "Presence" by its very definition requires someone else to be present with, which is why the Internal Revolution is never a one-person show. It takes place within you but always in the context of community as you live it out. Your Authentic Imprint isn't something you can build alone. Community and connection are vital to the process. Like an archeological team working on a dig, the real you is a treasure that you uncover in the presence of many who help you, encourage you, give you feedback, and challenge you.

The contrast is the performance-based leader focused on managing and manipulating outward perceptions. Presence-based leaders, however, pay attention to rich connections, authentic community, and worthwhile relationships. The first type of leadership is exhausting. Just ask Lisa. The second type can be energizing, as Rand and Lisa both now know.

The Presence-Based Brand Framework for Better Connection

Families, friendships, and Fortune 500 companies all operate much the same. Your presence is your brand. Everything else is just marketing. When you're looked to as the leader, people sense whether or not you're present, really present, with them. For example, children don't care whether you are the "perfect" mother or father, do they? As has been often said, children spell love T-I-M-E together. Kids want a real relationship with their parents, not a performance to impress other adults.

At work, teams can quickly sense when their leader is genuinely present, versus merely performing leadership roles. You can feel the difference in the room—whether someone is trying to manage perceptions or contributing real value. The goal is to identify more ways to lead from your strengths and less from what you think you *should* do or say in your role at work, among friends, in your community, at home—everywhere.

What if the biggest threat straining your leadership isn't competition or disruption, but the exhausting performance you put on every day? Studies show most leaders instinctively respond to persistent team challenges with external fixes—new programs, initiatives, or strategies—rather than the internal reflection and authentic growth that address root causes. They become so skilled at managing perceptions and demonstrating expertise that they lose touch with what made them effective leaders in the first place.

This isn't just a personal crisis—it's an organizational emergency. Research from Binghamton University and organizational psychology journals shows that authentic leadership—leaders being true to themselves and encouraging self-expression—significantly improves workplace culture, motivation, and employee engagement.[31]

Moving from performance to presence must be part of every Internal Revolution or it's incomplete. So how does that happen? In search of stronger connections, a deeper sense of community, and active engagement with others who share the same purpose and values, we must be willing to make the shift in these core elements:

From Perfect to Real.
From Impressive to Useful.
From Reactive to Responsive.
From Individual to Collaborative.

From Perfect to Real

What does it mean to be real, versus appearing perfect? Picture this. A brilliant CEO delivers a flawless presentation—every slide polished, every fact spot-on. But the room is distracted. Why? Because while her competence was clear, her connection to the people isn't. At work, a real leader shares their genuine thought process in search of a solution, instead of just polished conclusions. People don't follow your expertise—they follow your authentic conviction. It's not about better words. It's about real connection.

In our personal relationships, we begin by acknowledging that the perfect parent, or the perfect spouse, or the perfect friend doesn't exist, so we can stop desperately trying to create that illusion. The performance trap that we all sometimes find ourselves in is killing our influence on the world where we are called to fulfill our mission and do our greatest work. I challenge you to take one important conversation this week and focus entirely on being present. Focus on bringing authentic value to the conversation rather than managing how you're being perceived.

From Impressive to Useful

Choosing to be useful to people over trying to make an impression on everyone entails focusing on what serves others, rather than doing whatever we think makes us look good.

I was recently asked to lead a panel—a first for me. Naturally, I wanted it to be flawless, and I had a tempting moment where I considered trying to "prove myself" as a strong moderator. Then I paused and decided to lean into my real strengths instead. One,

I tapped into my strength that values individual connection. Two, I focused on my core value of building community wherever I am. So I scheduled intentional time with each speaker before the event—getting to know them not just as professionals, but as people. I also brought them together as a group to create shared clarity and connection ahead of time. Rather than trying to "look good" in a "look at me" moment, I focused on helping the others shine. The result? We had an engaging, energizing panel with meaningful insights—and the feedback was overwhelmingly positive. When you focus on serving others with your unique strengths, the good impression you want takes care of itself.

From Reactive to Responsive

Leading from your authentic core in the context of relationships makes you more responsive in times when your leadership is genuinely needed. Instead of kneejerk reactions to problems, you take your time to listen and respond in a way that honors your core values.

When a team member recently hit a rough patch, I felt that familiar urge to jump into action mode. But instead of reacting with assumptions or solutions, I paused and leaned once more into my strengths in paying attention to individuals and drew on my core value of being open and honest with others. So I took the time to understand what was really going on beneath the surface—and what they needed most. Then I customized a support plan that honored both their unique talents and the expectations of the role.

That conversation wasn't just about solving a problem and

moving on—it built trust, opened up honest dialogue, and allowed us both to grow. Being responsive doesn't mean doing more—it means leading with intention, grounded in who you truly are.

Listening isn't just waiting for your turn to talk. Instead of preparing your response while someone else is talking, be genuinely curious about perspectives you haven't considered.

Want to try it? In your next three conversations, resist the urge to immediately react to what's said. Instead, ask for more information. "Tell me more about that..." When someone shares an idea, find one element to get curious about before introducing any concerns. Practice saying: "I hadn't thought of it that way. What led you to that perspective?" The best ideas and solutions in our families and friendships and our organizations are often trapped inside people who don't feel genuinely heard.

From Individual to Collaborative

Being in community and connection with others requires us to move our thinking from individual to collaborative. Building a board of directors for your life is one of the most effective means of making this shift. Let me explain. Think of your personal board of directors as your professional dream team—a carefully selected group of virtual advisors who provide guidance, open doors, and help navigate personal and career challenges and transitions even before you need them.

As the leader in charge of your own Internal Revolution, a virtual board of directors can help you collaborate on the best ways to live in your strengths, lead from your core values, and accomplish your mission no matter what you are called to do.

It's virtual in the sense that you don't literally meet with these people as a group. Instead, you pick and choose whose strengths you can call on in the moments that matter most.

Let's take a deep dive on why collaborative thinking like this is essential to your Internal Revolution and explore how to accomplish it.

Identify Why and Where You Need More Connection

Malls and outdoor shopping centers often have kiosks with giant maps to show you "You Are Here" in relation to the other stores. This is your "You Are Here" spot on the map of your professional and personal leadership and impact where you review the Authentic Imprint formula: **(Strengths + Core Values + Mission) × Emotional Recognition = Your Authentic Imprint** and reflect on the four domains of your top strengths:

> **Executing** – Strengths that help you get things done
>
> **Influencing** – Strengths that help you lead and persuade others
>
> **Relationship Building** – Strengths that help you build strong relationships
>
> **Strategic Thinking** – Strengths that help you organize and plan

Unlike traditional one-on-one mentorship, a virtual personal board of directors leverages the power of multiple perspectives from experts in their fields. Therefore, it's important to know where you need to plug in certain people in your life to do two things: complement your strengths and challenge you at the same time. Reflect on how your top strengths currently influence your approach to leadership by reflecting on the following:

Which specific strengths do you rely on most when leading others?

Which ones are you not fully utilizing?

How do your strengths create both advantages and potential blind spots in your life and in your leadership?

In what situations do your strengths serve you well as a leader and help you make true impact? And when might they create challenges?

Strategic Pairing: Building a Balanced Board

Now consider how your strengths might interact with potential board members. Don't name names yet. At this point, just focus on job descriptions for board members whose own strengths will work in your favor. Think about how your natural strengths can be supported, stretched, or refined by others. The goal isn't to find your opposite—but rather to create productive tension and growth-oriented support. Look for people who:

- Complement your lesser-used domains
- Bring out the best in your natural talents
- Cover blind spots with wisdom and perspective
- Challenge you with care, not competition

The best boards don't just agree with you—they activate you. Look for the people who stretch your thinking, anchor your values, and call forth the most authentic version of who you are. Let's look at a few examples of strategic pairing:

If you naturally see patterns, possibilities, and future pathways...Pair with someone who thrives on action and momentum—someone who's wired to take that plan and run. They'll help you move from ideas to implementation.

If you're loyal, relationship-focused, and often avoid conflict...Bring in someone who is guided by strong values and conviction. They won't shy away from hard truths and can hold you accountable to what matters most—even when it's uncomfortable.

If you're highly driven and task-oriented...Pair with someone who is people-focused and who values growth over speed. They'll remind you to slow down and develop others—not just drive results.

If you love brainstorming and innovation, often generating idea after idea...Balance yourself with someone who thrives in structure and execution. They'll help turn your ideas into reality with systems and follow-through.

If you think deeply and process internally before making decisions...Find someone who is emotionally intuitive and people-attuned. They'll help you translate insights into connection—and challenge you to move out of your head and into the moment.

Your Dream Team

Imagine sitting at the head of an elegant conference table in a board room. There are empty chairs before you with name cards on the table at each place. These name cards represent the people on your board.

Your board of directors can be comprised of people who contribute to your personal wellbeing as well as your professional life, realizing that there may be some overlap of people who can benefit you in both areas.

Board Members Who Contribute to Your Personal Life

I suggest building these board members around Gallup's five interconnected dimensions of Wellbeing that we explored earlier in the book: Career, Social, Financial, Physical, and Community. Who can help you achieve a holistic sense of balance in each of these personal areas, either by providing a service, information and insight, advice, and/or a good example? Consider the following roles:

> **Career* Wellbeing:**
> *Liking what you do each day*
> **Potential board members:**
> Life coach – Someone who knows your goals and holds you accountable
> Spiritual/religious advisor – Someone like a priest, pastor, or teacher who will help you become healthy spiritually
> ***Having a Purpose**
>
> **Social Wellbeing:**
> *Maintaining meaningful relationships*
> **Potential board members:**

Professional counselor – Counseling can help you untangle relationship failures and issues
Friend mentor – An older and wiser adult who models how to maintain longterm friendships
Parent mentors – Whose parenting style do you admire? Think generationally. What can they teach you about parenting at every stage of life?

Financial Wellbeing:
Having enough of what you need
Potential board members:
Financial planner – Someone who can advise you regarding investing for the future
Attorney – Someone who can advise you with estate planning, wills, trusts, and other legal decisions that impact finances
Accountant – Someone who will help you with tax planning.

Physical Wellbeing:
Enjoying energy and health
Potential board members:
Medical doctor – Someone focuses on prevention and treatment
Physical trainer/exercise partner – Someone holding you accountable for regular exercise
(The role of a professional counselor can also fit here for mental health)

Community Wellbeing:

Being engaged and giving back

Potential board members:

Philanthropic mentor – Someone who models generous giving and can introduce you to opportunities to support good causes

Volunteer mentor – Someone who volunteers in an area you care about and can advise you on opportunities to volunteer your time

Board Members Who Help You in Your Career

These board members will primarily advise you regarding your career and professional goals. There are at least four roles you'll need:

- **Strategic Mentor**
  This is someone who's been where you're going. They have a big-picture understanding of career and life navigation. This person can help you spot patterns, avoid pitfalls, and identify high-leverage decisions. They're not in the weeds—they help you lift your head above the noise and see what really matters.

- **Executive Coach**
  Your executive coach helps you reflect inward and lead outward. They provide tools, questions, and frameworks to help you grow into the leader you're meant to be—not just professionally, but personally. They challenge you with care and champion your transformation with clarity.

- **Industry Expert**
  This person brings deep, relevant knowledge of your specific field. They help you stay sharp, see trends before others do, and navigate complex decisions with grounded insight. While others offer mindset or strategy, the industry expert brings timely know-how and credibility.

- **Peer Advisor**
  Your peer advisor is a trusted colleague walking a similar career path. They may not be ahead of you, but they offer perspective from the trenches. This is your sounding board—the one who understands the context, the pressure and the pace, and offers real-time feedback from a place of mutual respect.

If you're unsure about someone's strengths, observe their professional behavior and accomplishments. You may wish to review potential members' online presence, such as their LinkedIn profile, for clues about their approach and focus areas.

- Note what they seem naturally drawn to and energized by.
- What are they good at? What do other people say they're good at?
- Consider asking them directly about their strengths and preferences.

Choosing the Right Names

Now that you know what kind of people you're looking for, you're ready to start listing the names of specific individuals in your existing network who demonstrate the complementary strengths you need in your professional and personal life. If you don't currently know someone with the desired strengths, that's okay. Leave room to identify someone new in your circle of influence that you may not yet know.

Board Member Selection Criteria Checklist

For each potential board member, evaluate these areas:
- ☐ Proven success in target areas
- ☐ Complementary skill sets to yours
- ☐ Track record of mentoring others
- ☐ Shared values alignment
- ☐ Growth mindset and commitment
- ☐ Availability and accessibility
- ☐ Professional and/or personal chemistry
- ☐ Network reach and influence

The Smartest Person in the Room

The reason why community and connection matter in the Internal Revolution is simple. You have to find a way for your authentic self to connect emotionally in a way that matters to others. What good is it if you have finally discovered your true self—but no one else knows or understands or benefits from that person? What if no one is there following your leadership?

Sandy was the undisputed technical genius on her

engineering team. Twenty years of experience. Multiple patents. Everyone came to her for answers. So why did she feel completely invisible during leadership meetings?

"I present all the facts," she told me. "I show them exactly what needs to happen. But somehow my ideas never seem to land. Less experienced colleagues are getting buy-in for projects I should be leading." When I shadowed her through a week of meetings, I saw the problem. Sandy communicated like a technical manual. She led with data, buried the emotional stakes, and never connected her brilliant ideas to what mattered to her audience.

The turning point came when she applied the exponential power of emotional recognition in the Authentic Imprint formula for intentional daily living. What was lacking in Sandy was the ability to connect her mission and passion to real people and create positive influence through her authentic leadership design. Instead of starting her next proposal with market analysis, Sandy began the meeting with: "I've been thinking about why this problem keeps me up at night..." and shared her genuine concern about falling behind competitors.

Same data. Completely different impact.

Her proposal was approved unanimously. Two colleagues approached her afterward asking to collaborate. The difference? She stopped leading with her expertise (Strategic thinking domain) and started connecting with others through her heartfelt conviction about why the work matters to everyone (Relationship domain).

Notice when you're hiding behind data or your title instead of connecting with others through a common purpose. Showing and sharing your authentic conviction about why the work matters to people is what moves others to action.

Try this shift. Before your next important presentation at work or meaningful conversation with a close friend or family member, ask: "What's the emotional stake here—for me and for them?" That focus will help you connect you with people faster than anything else. Lead with why you care, then support it with what you know and the action that should be take.

The Compliment That Backfired Spectacularly

The words were out of my mouth before I realized how they sounded.

"Great job on the presentation, Jeff. You seemed so much more confident than usual!"

Jeff's smile froze. More confident than usual? I had meant it as encouragement. But what he'd heard was: "You're normally not confident, and we all notice." I meant to be supportive. Jeff experienced it as an inadvertent reveal of how I'd been perceiving him all along.

I have since started paying attention to what I call "emotional wake"—the feeling people are left with after interacting with the real me. That's the "impression" element of our definition: **Your Authentic Imprint is the unmistakable energy and authenticity you bring—whether in person or online—the living, breathing impression you leave on others, day after day. It's not about being more impressive, but about being more you.**

"Encouragement" that comes with subtle undertones of surprise when team members performed well is not exactly uplifting! I was unintentionally communicating that I carried low expectations. Instead of "You seemed so much more confident!" I started saying: "I really appreciated how you handled the Q&A section. Your responses were thoughtful and clear."

Same positive intention. Completely different emotional impact.

After every important conversation this week, ask yourself: "What feeling did I likely leave that person with?" Leadership isn't just about what you intend to communicate—it's about the emotional patterns you create that people learn to navigate around when interacting with your authentic self.

Who You Always Wanted to Be

Regularly spending time in community and having daily connection with others, especially those closest to you, will serve as reliable test-labs for your authentic self as you work on becoming who you were meant to be.

As you begin your own Internal Revolution, remember it takes a village. So pay attention to that "village" around you. Who speaks truth to you? Who celebrates your authentic self? Who challenges you to grow? The revolution isn't a solo journey—it's a community transformation. When you lead from the inside out, you give others permission to do the same. That's how we change the world: one authentic leader at a time, supported by communities that believe in who we're becoming, not just who we've been.

As I said at the beginning, everyone's Internal Revolution is unique, but there are certain unifying outcomes and milestones that characterize every revolutionary. In their own individual journeys, the growing community of revolutionaries is ever transforming along a similar path. Look back on your path and see how far you've come after reading this book:

- **Are you moving from Confused to Clear?**
  Revolutionaries navigate their path with newfound clarity and direction regarding their strengths, core values, and mission.

- **Are you moving from Lacking Purpose to Purposeful?**
  Revolutionaries are discovering and embracing their true, guiding purpose every day.

- **Are you moving from Isolated to Connected?**
  Revolutionaries forge connections that empower their leadership.

When you commit to showing up in life as yourself, you join a community of revolutionaries whose collective energy is free from filtering and whose true value is seen and recognized by others. Together, our band of revolutionaries is stronger because we know what it takes to live intentionally every day.

True impact in life stems from this kind of deeply rooted alignment. When your everyday actions reflect your inner core, you will naturally attract opportunities and influence others. While many people will continue to depend on others' approval and look outside themselves for identity, you are well on your way now to knowing more about the inner you. Not your titles. Not your achievements. You.

The Internal Revolution has never been about doing more. It's much more difficult than that because it's about being more—more of who you truly are. If you're at a point in your life where you've achieved success on paper, but something still feels off, you're the perfect candidate for the Internal Revolution. Keep moving. When the pressure is constant, the title is heavy, and somewhere along the way you've lost touch with the part of you that once felt energized, clear, and deeply fulfilled—keep going. What you've learned in this book is your invitation to come home to yourself.

How you lead, how you live, and how you show up in the world—it's all on the table in a revolution so extraordinary that it can change your life and work forever. Right now, you have all that you need to rediscover your authentic strengths and values and align with your true mission in life. When changes come, and they will, you can navigate them with clarity and calm, leading yourself and those you have responsibility for from the center of your authentic self.

As it turns out, you didn't need a new strategy in order to lead with purpose, peace, and powerful presence. You just needed a new starting point—one that begins within you.

The Heart of the Revolutionary

You've always been the steady one.
The one others rely on. The one who rises to the challenge, no matter what's on your plate. You've built a strong career, achieved remarkable things, and wear your title with pride. But lately... something's shifted.

You're starting to feel it—beneath the meetings, the metrics, and the momentum.

A quiet question rising inside: Is this really who I am? Or just who I've been expected to be?

You've reached a point in your leadership where more success, more structure, or more productivity just isn't enough.

Because what you're really craving isn't more achievement. It's alignment.

You want clarity.

You want peace.

You want to stop performing and start leading from who you truly are—not just the role you've been trained to play.

And I see you. Because I've been there too.

I know the pressure of being the go-to person, the decision-maker, the face of responsibility. I know how easily our identities can get tied up in titles and external validation. And I also know how liberating it is to finally say:

I'm ready to come home to myself.

That's what this movement is about.

It's not about burning everything down or walking away from leadership.

It's about doing the internal work to rediscover your strengths, reconnect with your purpose, and lead from your values—every single day.

It's an **Internal Revolution.**

And when you do this work—when you begin to live from the inside out—you transform not only your life, but the lives of everyone around you. Your family. Your team. Your organization. Your legacy.

You don't need another performance improvement plan.
You don't need to check more boxes.
You just need space to remember who you are beneath the noise.

Let's create that space together.

You don't have to do this alone.
There's a roadmap. There's a journal. There are connection points with like-minded leaders. And there is a place of support awaiting the real you.

The you that's not just respected... but centered.
Not just productive... but at peace.
Not just successful... but fulfilled.

You don't need to be more productive.
You need to be more you.

Let's begin.

∼

Worth Remembering:
Join the movement. Lead the revolution.
Your people don't need a better version of your title.
They need you.

PUTTING IT INTO PRACTICE

QUESTIONS FOR REFLECTION

1. Who has helped you become your authentic self?
2. Who do you need to add to your personal board of directors?
3. Where can you plug into your community to serve others on a regular basis?
4. What is your definition of connection?

EXERCISE 1

Write a Letter to Your Future Self: Outline how you plan to leverage your top five strengths for the rest of this year to achieve the following three goals:

> Live in Your Strengths.
> Dominate your Day.
> Transform Your Life.

Describe how each strength can enhance your personal and professional brand and support these goals for growth.

EXERCISE 2

You're not alone in this journey. Connect with fellow revolutionaries at danawilliamsco.com and follow the Dominate Your Day podcast at **www.danawilliamsco.com/dominate-your-day-podcast** for ongoing inspiration from other difference makers.

RESOURCES

QUICK REFERENCE GUIDE

Your Authentic Imprint™
Your Authentic Imprint is the unmistakable energy and authenticity you bring—whether in person or online—the living, breathing impression you leave on others, day after day. It's not about being more impressive, but about being more you.

Your Authentic Imprint formula for intentional daily living:

(Strengths + Core Values + Mission) × Emotional Recognition = Your Authentic Imprint

Your Internal Revolution™
The Internal Revolution is the internal work necessary to rediscover your authentic strengths, lead from your core values, and reconnect with your true purpose—every single day.

Strengths: Your unique talents, skills, and qualities that energize and empower you.
Core Values: The guiding beliefs or principles that matter most to you and shape your decisions.

Mission: Your sense of purpose—what drives you and gives your life meaning.

Emotional Recognition: Your ability to identify, understand, and respond to your own feelings and those of others.

Four Strengths Domains:

- **Executing:** Get things done
- **Influencing:** Lead and persuade
- **Relationship Building:** Build relationships
- **Strategic Thinking:** Organize and plan

Five Elements of Wellbeing:

1. **Career Wellbeing:** Liking what you do each day*
2. **Social Wellbeing:** Maintaining meaningful relationships
3. **Financial Wellbeing:** Having enough of what you need
4. **Physical Wellbeing:** Enjoying energy and health
5. **Community Wellbeing:** Being engaged and giving back

(*I broaden to having a "Purpose")

Daily Emotional Recognition Practice:

- **Morning Check-In:** "What energy am I bringing to strategic work today?" (Level 1)
- **Real-time Awareness:** "What does this situation need from me?" (Level 2)
- **Evening Reflection:** "What did I leave people with regarding our strategic direction?" (Level 3)

Goal: Not perfection, but presence. Responsive leadership instead of reactive management.

Mission Statement vs. Authentic Imprint™

Mission Statement	Authentic Imprint™
Concise, actionable, daily "North Star"	Holistic self-leadership and energy model (for Personal Brand)
Focus: Who/How/What impact you serve	Focus: Who you are, what energizes you, and how you lead
Use: Daily decisions, clarity, inspiration	Use: Deep self-reflection, energy management, leadership

- **Mission Statement:** Use for clear direction, daily decision-making, and as your quick purpose statement.
- **Authentic Imprint™:** Use for holistic self-mastery, integrating strengths, values, purpose, and emotional self-awareness to maximize authentic impact.

AVAILABLE FROM DANA WILLIAMS

<u>www.danawilliamsco.com</u>

Visit Dana Williams Co. online to explore a variety of resources to support your Internal Revolution.

Receive Your Authentic Imprint (Free Assessment) – Are you a difference maker who wants to lead authentically and transform from within? Based on the principles covered in *The Internal Revolution*, discover your authentic leadership profile and get your personalized roadmap for making a greater impact through this quick 3-minute assessment.

danawilliamsco.scoreapp.com

Listen to the Dominate Your Day Podcast – The Dominate Your Day podcast is for leaders looking to make a difference in their careers and communities. In each episode, hear from difference makers who have transformed their lives from the inside out to make an impact on the world. Listen on Apple or Spotify.

www.danawilliamsco.com/dominate-your-day-podcast

Subscribe to the Weekly Leader's Digest – Each week we'll email you easy action items you can incorporate into your daily work routine to help you become a better leader.

www.danawilliamsco.com/weekly-leaders-digest

Order The Strengths Journal – The only Gallup-certified licensed daily planner that helps you actively use your strengths to dominate your day and ultimately transform your life.

thestrengthsjournal.com

CONNECT WITH US

Connect with Dana on social media for access to strategies on how to Live in Your Strengths, Dominate Your Day, and Transform Your Life. Additionally, book a discovery call at www.danawilliamsco.com to see how Dana Willams Co. can help leaders and teams work from their strengths, align with a common mission, and reclaim their purpose.

LinkedIn: www.linkedin.com/in/danawilliams2/
Instagram: www.instagram.com/danawilliamsconsulting
Facebook: www.facebook.com/danawilliamsconsulting

ENDNOTES

1   https://www.gallup.com/workplace/237020/five-essential-elements.
    aspx

2   https://www.wbfinder.com/help/general/247874/five-essential-
    elements-wellbeing.aspx

3   https://www.csus.edu/administration-business-affairs/human-
    resources/learning-development/_internal/_documents/five-
    elements-workshop-materials.pdf

4   https://www.wbfinder.com/help/general/247874/five-essential-
    elements-wellbeing.aspx

5   https://www.gallup.com/workplace/215924/well-being.aspx

6   https://www.wbfinder.com/help/general/247874/five-essential-
    elements-wellbeing.aspx

7   https://www.csus.edu/administration-business-affairs/human-
    resources/learning-development/_internal/_documents/five-
    elements-workshop-materials.pdf

8   https://store.gallup.com/p/en-us/10410/wellbeing%3A-the-five-
    essential-elements?c=5

9   https://www.gallup.com/workplace/237020/five-essential-elements.
    aspx

10 *Mindset: The New Psychology of Success*, Carol Dweck, Ballantine
    Books, 2007.

11 *Chatter: The Voice in Our Head, Why It Matters, and How to Harness It,* Dr. Ethan Kross, Crown, 2021.

12 As told in an interview with Lynne Rosetto Kasper, host of the Splendid Table, https://www.splendidtable.org/story/2013/08/02/julia-child-on-cooking-that-was-really-what-id-been-looking-for-all-my-life

13 https://www.gallup.com/workplace/285674/improve-employee-engagement-workplace.aspx#:~:text=People%20want%20purpose%20and%20meaning,work%20than%20they%20used%20to.

14 https://prologue.blogs.archives.gov/2021/03/11/taking-it-to-the-stars-eileen-collins-space-shuttle-commander/, March 11, 2021, Jessie Kratz.

15 https://ntrs.nasa.gov/citations/20190026642

16 Gartner, "Change Fatigue: 71% of Employees Overwhelmed by Change at Work," 2023.

17 McKinsey & Company, "Change fatigue: What is it—and how can organizations address it?" 2023.

18 Neuroscientist and author Dr. Caroline Leaf has excellent suggestions for this daily habit in her book, *Cleaning Up Your Mental Mess.*

19 https://www.hbs.edu/ris/Publication%20Files/mogilner%20norton%202016_951db108-1099-4482-8b02-27eed5e2a87e.pdf

20 https://www.tfhd.com/news/health-benefits-of-volunteering-live-longer-and-thrive/

21 Hsu et al., 2005; Rushworth & Behrens, 2008; Yu & Dayan, 2005.

22 (Baumeister et al., 1998; Inzlicht & Schmeichel, 2012).

23 (Bridges, 2009; Fisher, 2011).

24 *Waiting on God*, Andrew Murray, Whitaker House, 1983.

25 Proverbs 3:5-6

26 https://www.mckinsey.com/featured-insights/mckinsey-explainers/what-is-decision-making

27   https://irp-cdn.multiscreensite.com/fb082353/files/uploaded/
      The%20Authenticity%20Paradox%20HBR.pdf

28   *Harvard Business Review*, Discovering Your Authentic Leadership,
      Bill George, Peter Sims, Andrew N. McLean, Diana Mayer, February
      2007.

29   https://pmc.ncbi.nlm.nih.gov/articles/PMC4911781/

30   Walumbwa, F. O., et al. (2008). Authentic leadership: Development
      and validation of a theory-based measure, *Journal of Management*,
      34(1), 89-126.

31   https://www.binghamton.edu/news/story/5328/new-research-
      authentic-leadership-improving-workplace